Walking With Purpose · Young Adult Bible Studies

GOD'S LOVE IN THREE-PART HARMONY

Walking with the Lord is a journey that lasts a lifetime. If you enjoyed the *Opening Your Heart Series*, look out for these new Bible studies that will continue to nurture your soul.

THE KEEPING IN BALANCE SERIES

Harmony – Part I
How to find the balance between mediocrity and perfectionism and become the woman God created you to be without stressing.

Perspective – Part II
Become more content and grow stronger in the face of failure, and keep moving when you're tempted to settle for the status quo.

Exhale – Part III
Ideas for establishing a rhythm of rest, worship, and surrender and reorder your thoughts to create inner peace.

COMING SOON

THE DISCOVERING OUR DIGNITY SERIES

Tapestry – Part I
From relationship challenges, to the death of dreams, and the lure of compromise– how to apply age-old wisdom from the women of Genesis to the challenges of today.

Legacy – Part II
Explore a myriad of women's issues such as shame, loneliness, and making a difference in the world, and learn from the wisdom of ancient women.

Heritage – Part III
Inspiration about work and worship from key women in the New Testament, including Mary, the Blessed Mother, and her insights on what it means to live sacrificially.

For more spiritual inspiration or to learn more about Walking With Purpose, visit us at walkingwithpurpose.com

walking with purpose

You're also invited to join our community on Facebook, Twitter, Pinterest and Instagram.

walking with purpose

Dear friend,

Welcome to *Exhale*, part III of the *Keeping in Balance* young adult Bible study series! I'm so glad you are taking the time to open your Bible and delve into the rich teachings and encouragement that God has for you there. We are promised in Isaiah 55:11 that God's word doesn't go out void— it always achieves the purpose that God intended for it. I claim that promise for you and pray that His words would travel to your heart with pinpoint accuracy— going to the places where you most need to hear His voice.

In a world that longs for comfort and often settles for superficiality, your hunger for truth and holiness sets you apart. I wish that your desire to grow closer to God meant that the enemy of your soul would just give up and leave you alone. But I know that nothing scares him more than a woman who knows her true identity as a beloved daughter of God, and he is terrified of one who is willing to engage into the spiritual battle. The more seriously you take your faith, the more he'd tempt you to settle for mediocrity.

Because of that reality…
I pray that you would exhale any sense of powerlessness— the feeling that nothing will ever change. May you inhale the spirit of hope.

May you exhale any sense of complacency that wants to settle where it's comfortable. I pray you would inhale passion for holiness.

May you exhale any religiosity which might tempt you to equate outward religious appearance with inward conversion. May you inhale God's grace.

I pray most of all that God would have your heart— that most precious part of you. May He meet you in that hidden place, bringing balance, rest, and peace.

With love and prayers for you,
Lisa Brenninkmeyer
Founder and Chief Purpose Officer of Walking with Purpose

Exhale
Keeping in Balance Series
Part III

www.walkingwithpurpose.com

Authored by Lisa Brenninkmeyer
Cover and page design by True Cotton
Production management by Christine Welsko

IMPRIMATUR + William E. Lori, S.T.D., Archbishop of Baltimore

The recommended Bible translations for use in Blaze and Walking with Purpose studies are: The New American Bible, which is the translation used in the United States for the readings at Mass; The Revised Standard Version, Catholic Edition; and The Jerusalem Bible.

Any internet addresses (websites, blogs, etc.) in this book are offered as a resource and may change in the future. Please refer to www.walkingwithpurpose.com as the central location for corresponding materials and references.

Printed: November 2018

ISBN: 978-1-943173-24-2

Keeping in Balance Series, Part III

TABLE OF CONTENTS

INTRODUCTION

LESSONS

APPENDICES

ANSWER KEY

PRAYER PAGES

NOTES

Welcome to Walking with Purpose

You have many choices when it comes to how you spend your time—thank you for choosing Walking with Purpose. Studying God's Word with an open and receptive heart will bring spiritual growth and enrichment to all aspects of your life, making every moment that you've invested well worth it.

Each one of us comes to this material from our own unique vantage point. You are welcome as you are. No previous experience is necessary. Some of you will find that the questions in this study cause you to think about concepts that are new to you. Others might find much is a review. God meets each one of us where we are, and He is always faithful, taking us to a deeper, better place spiritually, regardless of where we begin.

The Structure of *Keeping in Balance* Series

The *Keeping in Balance* series is a three-part Bible study, each of which can stand alone, or all three can be completed one after the other. Each Bible study integrates Scripture with the teachings of the Roman Catholic Church to point us to principles that help us manage life's pace and pressure while living with calm and steadiness.

This Bible study can be used on your own, giving you great material for daily Scripture meditation and prayer. It also lends itself well to group discussion. We encourage you to gather your tribe—a handful of friends who want more out of their spiritual lives. The accountability and deeper friendship that will result make it so much easier to live out the truths contained in these pages.

Study Guide Format and Reference Materials

The three parts of *Exhale - Keeping in Balance Part III* are divided into three sections:

The first section comprises six lessons, which are divided into five "days" to help you form a habit of reading and reflecting on God's Word regularly. If you are a young woman who has only bits and pieces of time throughout your day to accomplish tasks, you will find this breakdown of the lessons especially helpful. Each day focuses on Scripture readings and related teaching passages, and ends with a Quiet Your Heart reflection, which should lead you to a time of personal prayer. In addition, Day Five includes a Saint's Story; a lesson conclusion; a resolution section, in which you set a goal for yourself based on a theme of the lesson; and short clips from the

Catechism of the Catholic Church, which are referenced throughout the lesson to complement the Scripture study.

The second section, the appendices, contains supplemental materials referred to during the study.

The third section contains the answer key. You will benefit so much more from the Bible study if you work through the questions on your own, searching your heart, as this is your very personal journey of faith. The answer key is meant to enhance small group discussion and provide personal guidance or insight when needed.

A memory verse has been chosen for each part of the *Keeping in Balance* series, and we encourage you to memorize it as you move through the Bible study. An illustration of the verse can be found in the Introduction section, and a color version and phone lock screen can be downloaded from our website.

At the end of the book are pages on which to write weekly prayer intentions.

Walking with Purpose™ Young Adult Bible Studies

The *Opening Your Heart* Series

Beloved: *Opening Your Heart, Part I* is a six-lesson Bible study that lays a strong foundation for our true identity as beloved daughters of God. We'll learn that we belong to a family that will never abandon us. We'll encounter grace and practical tools to make God our first priority. Jesus will meet us personally in the pages of His Word, and we'll be transformed as a result.

Unshaken: *Opening Your Heart, Part II* is a six-lesson Bible study that fills our spiritual toolbox with exactly what we need to grow stronger in our faith. We'll discuss why and how we should read the Bible, what difference the sacraments really make in our lives, how to bravely face challenges in our efforts to follow Christ, and the way Mary perfectly mothers us through it all.

Steadfast: *Opening Your Heart, Part III,* a six-lesson Bible study, unpacks why we are hustling for our worth and how to conquer our fears. We'll look at the role of suffering and forgiveness in our lives, and dig deeper into how we can truly change in the areas where we have felt enslaved. We'll explore life purpose, our vocations, and the depth of God's personal love for His beloved children.

The *Keeping in Balance* Series

Harmony: *Keeping in Balance, Part I* is a five-lesson Bible study that helps us to get a grip on our lives by looking at the importance of authenticity, setting priorities, managing expectations, and having healthy relationships. We'll also explore finding a balance between mediocrity and perfectionism so that we can become the women God created us to be without stressing or striving.

Perspective: *Keeping in Balance, Part II* is a five-lesson Bible study that addresses how we can become more content, grow stronger in areas where we've failed a million times, and get moving when we feel like settling for the status quo. *Perspective* also explores how we can engage our culture as Catholics at a time when the reputation of Christians is at an all-time low.

Exhale: *Keeping in Balance, Part III* is a six-lesson Bible study that helps us establish a rhythm of rest, worship, and surrender. If you long for more simplicity in your life and are ready to order your thoughts so you can experience inner peace, this Bible study will both inspire you and provide you with practical steps to make positive changes.

The *Discovering Our Dignity* Series: *Coming Soon*

Tapestry: Discovering Our Dignity, Part I is a six-lesson Bible study that explores the beginning of salvation history through the eyes of the women of Genesis. The difficulties they struggled with are remarkably similar to our own: relationship challenges, the death of dreams, the lure of compromise, and the danger of self-reliance. We'll learn from their mistakes as we apply age-old wisdom to our modern challenges.

Legacy: Discovering Our Dignity, Part II is a nine-lesson Bible study that picks up where *Tapestry* left off. Our exploration of the women of salvation history continues as we move further into the Old Testament. We'll explore a myriad of women's issues such as loneliness, shame, leadership challenges, and making a difference in the world.

Heritage: Discovering Our Dignity, Part III is a seven-lesson Bible Study that highlights key women of the New Testament. Mary and Martha will help us explore the balance of work and worship, and the poor widow will shed new light on what it means to live sacrifically. We'll be inspired especially by Mary, the Blessed Mother, as we apply her wisdom to our daily challenges.

WE ARE THE
CLAY &
you are our
POTTER
we are all
THE WORK OF
your hand

Isaiah 64:7

✳ walking with purpose

---

[1] Full-Color Free Printables available at walkingwithpurpose.com/free-printables

Walking with Purpose™ Website

Please visit our website at www.walkingwithpurpose.com to find supplemental materials that complement our Bible studies; a link to our online store for additional Bible studies, DVDs, books, and more; and the following free content:

WWP Scripture Printables of our exclusively designed verse cards that complement all Bible studies. Available in various sizes, lock screens for phones, and a format that allows you to e-mail them to friends.

WWP Bible Study Playlists of Lisa's favorite music to accompany each Bible study.

WWP Videos of all Connect Coffee Talks by Lisa Brenninkmeyer.

WWP Blog by Lisa Brenninkmeyer, a safe place where you are welcome, where the mask can drop and you can be real. Subscribe for updates.

WWP Leadership Development Program

We are here to help you take your leadership to the next level! Through our training, you'll discover insights that help you achieve your leadership potential. You'll be empowered to step out of your comfort zone and experience the rush of serving God with passion and purpose. We want you to know that you are not alone; we offer you encouragement and the tools you need to reach out to a world that desperately needs to experience the love of God.

Links to WWP Social Media

Twitter, Pinterest, Facebook, Instagram

Lessons

 NOTES

Lesson 1

BALANCE THROUGH WORSHIP

Introduction

"To worship is to quicken the conscience by the holiness of God, to feed the mind with the truth of God, to purge the imagination by the beauty of God, to open the heart to the love of God, to devote the will to the purpose of God." —William Temple

A quote like that gives us an inkling that perhaps worship involves a little more than getting our bodies into a church pew on Sunday. What William Temple describes sounds like it involves all we are and all we have. And he's right.

Worship is more than good liturgy, or great music, or eloquent prayers. It's really about a human heart opening up and reaching out to connect with God. It's a turning of the face to soak up the richness of who God is. It's pouring out our love to God (however imperfectly it might be done), knowing that He receives what we give with open arms. It's basking in His presence. Worship is about intimacy.

And it sounds good, in theory. But then we have to stop for gas on the way to Mass and we arrive late, the homily's lame, the music is dismal, and everyone looks old. So we quickly conclude that this kind of worship must be for a select few who are destined for beatification, but not for the rest of us, who are doing a countdown of how many songs are left in the Mass.

So what should we do? Give up? Coast along? Be grateful that no one can read our thoughts, so no one's the wiser if we mindlessly rush through our prayers and daydream during Mass?

These questions make me think about a wonderful book called *The 5 Love Languages*, by Gary Chapman. In it, he explains that each of us has a preferred way of receiving love: through acts of service, words of affirmation, receiving gifts, physical touch, or quality time. If we want to effectively love someone, we're wise to find out which of those expressions of love is most meaningful to him or her. But if we look at it as an obligation, as one of the many things we have to do (sigh), then the other person probably won't feel very loved, regardless of which love language is spoken.

So what is God's love language? Because God desires intimacy and connection with us, I'd guess that quality time is pretty important to Him. And that's another way to look at worship. It's quality time that we offer to God, because we want Him to know that we love Him. But we don't want to come to Him out of obligation. That's better than nothing, but as far as motivations go, it's not what we're aiming for. The truth is, we need God's help to love Him well. So let's ask for that help, so our worship becomes our way of telling God that He has our hearts.

"We love, because He first loved us." (1 John 4:19)

Day One
REALITY CHECK

1. If you were asked to stop and pray right now, you would perhaps make the sign of the cross, probably close your eyes, and start saying something. Our prayers are filled with words, and more often than not, the words are about us. "Can you help me with this, God? And these are the needs of the people I love." There is definitely nothing wrong with going to God with our needs; in fact, we are told to do that very thing. But is it possible that at times, our words get in the way of our worship? What would happen if we stopped talking for a little while (don't panic—I'm not saying *forever*), and instead took a long look at God? Read each of the following verses, and instead of preparing to write an answer, just think about the truth contained in each one. Allow the verses to help you to contemplate the greatness of God.

   Exodus 34:6

   Psalm 19:1–4

Psalm 102:13, 26–28 NAB

When we worship, we are focusing on *who God is*, not *what He gives*.

2. Does God command us to worship (Matthew 4:10) because He needs it? See Acts 17:24–25.[2]

3. Colossians 1:16 tells us, "For in [God] were created all things in heaven and on earth . . . all things were created through him and for him." Do you think we often act as if God was created for us—to do what we want Him to do, to bless us and those we love?

Worship gets us in a posture in which we recognize that God doesn't owe us an explanation. Because He is the Creator and Sustainer of the universe, He has the right to do whatever He pleases.

4. Distrust in God will get in the way of our worshipping Him. What do we learn from Isaiah 55:8–9 regarding our ability to understand why God wills and allows certain things?

---

[2] When Acts 17:24 states that God does not dwell in sanctuaries made by human hands, it does not mean that God is not present in our parishes and tabernacles. It means that He is not limited by a physical dwelling.

"To put it bluntly, when you get your own universe, you can make your own standards. When we disagree, let's not assume it's [God's] reasoning that needs correction."[3] —Francis Chan

Quiet your heart and enjoy His presence. . . . Meditate on who He is.

"What comes into our minds when we think about God is the most important thing about us. . . . Worship is pure or base as the worshipper entertains high or low thoughts of God. For this reason the gravest question before the Church is always God Himself, and the most portentous fact about any man is not what he at a given time may say or do, but what he in his deep heart conceives God to be like."[4] —A. W. Tozer

Take a few moments to examine your heart. Are there circumstances (past or present) that make no sense to you, and as a result, you've been frustrated with God and have questioned His goodness? Is this getting in the way of your ability to love Him? Confess any pride that has led you to a sense that God owes you an explanation. Ask Him for the humility to trust Him even when you don't understand Him.

Day Two
INVITED IN

Note: Throughout the Old Testament and when Jesus walked the earth, the Jewish people went to the temple to worship God. There were three parts to the temple: the courts, the Holy Place (where only priests were allowed to enter), and the Holy of Holies. God dwelt in the innermost part of the temple, the Holy of Holies. This sacred place was behind a thick blue, purple, and scarlet veil. Once a year, the high priest was allowed past that veil, but he had to enter with a blood sacrifice, and only for the purpose of asking forgiveness for the sins of his people.[5] No one else could enter. This veil was six inches thick and sixty feet high, and it has been said that if a horse were tethered to each corner and they ran in opposite directions, the veil would not tear. It was an imposing curtain that communicated, loud and clear, GOD IS HOLY, AND YOU ARE NOT. YOU MAY NOT APPROACH HIM. The people weren't prepared to meet God, so the veil both prevented them from entering and protected them.

---

[3] Francis Chan and Danae Yankosky, *Crazy Love: Overwhelmed by a Relentless God* (Colorado Springs: David C. Cook, 2008), 34.

[4] A. W. Tozer, *The Knowledge of the Holy* (San Francisco: Harper San Francisco, 1992), 1.

[5] Leviticus 16:1–35.

1. Who is the one person who was allowed to see God's glory? Describe how that occurred. See Exodus 33:18–23.

2. When he came down from seeing God's glory and spending forty days in His presence, Moses spoke to the Israelite community about what had happened. What did he do when he finished speaking with them? See Exodus 34:29–33.

3. What happened when Christ was dying on the cross? See Matthew 27:50–51. What do you believe is the significance of this?

The veil symbolized the separation of man and God because of man's sin. But when Jesus died in our place, paying the price for our sins, a divine exchange took place. He took our sins on Himself, and now offers us His righteousness in exchange. "For our sake, he made him to be sin who did not know sin, so that we might become the righteousness of God in him." (2 Corinthians 5:21) Because of Jesus, we can now enter the Holy of Holies and be in God's presence. "Through the blood of Jesus we have confidence of entrance into the sanctuary by the new and living way he opened for us through the veil, that is, his flesh." (Hebrews 10:19–20)

4. Jesus offers us this divine exchange of our sin for His righteousness as a free gift. But it's up to us to receive it. Read Appendix 3 Conversion of Heart. Have you experienced conversion of heart? The veil has been torn and you are being invited into the Holy of Holies. Journal your thoughts below.

Quiet your heart and enjoy His presence. . . . You're being invited behind the veil.

If you can, spend some time in adoration of the Eucharist today. Meditate on how different it is to worship God today with complete access to His presence compared with how the Israelite people experienced Him in the Old Testament.

If you can't get to adoration, be assured, God is present with you now. The veil has been torn. He invites you in. How will you respond?

Day Three
TRANSFORMED

Read 2 Corinthians 3:12–18.

1. What happens whenever a person turns to the Lord? See 2 Corinthians 3:16.

2. What happens when we gaze on the Lord's glory with an unveiled face? See 2 Corinthians 3:18.

3. Do you want to be transformed? If so, what would you like to see changed about yourself? List your thoughts below, in the form of a prayer, asking God to transform you.

Dear God,

4. What unique experiences of gazing on the Lord's glory are offered in the Catholic Church? See CCC 1123 and CCC 1380.

Quiet your heart and enjoy His presence. . . . Let Him transform you from the inside out.

Prayer might not always change my circumstances, but it always holds the possibility of changing me. I often begin my prayer time with a focus on all I need and lack. But when I am able to shift my eyes to the way Jesus has suffered for me and proven his love for me, something changes. I'm reminded of the possibility that he knows what is best for me, and that may or may not be what I am currently longing for. I am transformed from within as I learn to trust God's provision, timing, and methods. Fixing my eyes on Jesus and asking him to transform my desires to better reflect his own brings the transformation that I hunger for.

He is inviting you and me to come into his presence with unveiled faces. This means that he wants the real you and the real me- not the fake fine we might present to others. We can come into his presence broken, and we are guaranteed to leave blessed.

Day Four
GLORY TO YOU, OH LORD

Worship requires that we take our eyes off of ourselves. It serves as a reminder that it's not about us. Could it be that when we feel it's hard to worship at Mass because of poor music or a less than interesting homily, our focus is in the wrong place? If Jesus promises that He will show up (and He always fulfills this promise in the Eucharist), don't we have all that we need in order to worship Him? Great music and inspiring homilies help prepare and challenge us (and that's always a good thing), but when they are absent, we aren't prevented from worshipping.

Read Revelation 4:8–11.

Note: *Revelation* means "a lifting of the veil."

1. When we celebrate Mass, we are joining those who are celebrating the liturgy in heaven. Think about that. Our worship is being lifted up and joined to theirs. Revelation 4:8–11 lifts the veil and gives us a glimpse of what worship is like in heaven. Which part of the passage reminds you of Mass?

2. What is the posture of the saints (the twenty-four elders) before God? What do they cast down before God's throne? See Revelation 4:10.

The twenty-four elders "represent the saints, who are dressed like priests [in white] and kings [with crowns]."[6] All baptized Christians are united with Christ, and share in His mission as a priest, prophet, and king. As a daughter of the King, you, too, wear a crown.

---

[6] *Ignatius Catholic Study Bible: New Testament*, 2nd Catholic ed., RSV (San Francisco: Ignatius Press, 2010), 498.

3. At the end of Saint Paul's life, he wrote about the reward he would receive in heaven for his perseverance on earth. How was this reward described? See 2 Timothy 4:6–8.

4. The "crown of righteousness" is a reward for good deeds that is *only* possible because of God working in and through us. As Jesus said, "I am the vine, you are the branches. Whoever remains in me and I in him will bear much fruit, because without me you can do nothing." (John 15:5) As a beautiful act of humility, what can you prayerfully cast before the throne as an act of worship?

Quiet your heart and enjoy His presence. . . . Bow before His greatness.

"Not to us, Lord, not to us but to your name give glory because of your mercy and faithfulness." (Psalm 115:1)

It's human nature to seek glory for ourselves. If we question whether this is true, we only need to experience someone else getting credit for something we have done. Can you offer God the credit for any good in you? When we lay even our good deeds at His feet, our hands are empty and free to be lifted in praise.

Day Five
HOLY EXPECTANCY

Every moment of the day can be an act of worship. Does that sound impossible? I'm not suggesting that you spend all your time in a church; rather, that you live with the awareness that God is always by your side. No matter what is going on in your life, you can always turn your heart toward Him.

When we lift our faces to God with a spirit of expectancy, we are continually looking for opportunities to connect with Him. Miracles will flow out of that intimate relationship. Supernatural strength will be given. Time will be stretched. Healing will take place.

1. How are we told to pray in 1 Thessalonians 5:17?

Does this instruction seem impossible? Saint Paul wasn't suggesting that we spend every minute on our knees. "Praying without ceasing" means that we live with a steady awareness of our dependency on God. We thank Him for the good things that come our way, whisper frequent requests for help, and stay conscious of the fact that everything we say and do can be either an offering of worship or a step away from God. As we go through the day, we can ask God, over and over again, "What would you like me to do in this minute?" This is an act of worship.

2. We can pray and worship God in the midst of our activities, but there's also great benefit in turning off the noise and sitting in silence. A Desert Father, Ammonas, wrote, "Behold, my beloved. I have shown you the power of silence, how thoroughly it heals and how fully pleasing it is to God. . . . It is by silence that the saints grew . . . it was because of silence that the power of God dwelt in them, because of silence that the mysteries of God were known to them."[7] When do you experience silence? If it's missing in your life, what can you do to carve out time for quiet worship?

God wants to speak to us; we just can't hear Him. Because of this, when we quiet our hearts and sit silently in His presence, we can have a holy expectancy that we will hear from Him. It's unlikely that He will speak in an audible voice, but He speaks through Scripture and also through impressing things on our hearts. He may bring to mind a person He'd like you to pray for, or give you insight into a problem you face. If you have taken time to memorize Scripture, He will often speak His own words into your heart, offering comfort and guidance.

---

[7] Thomas Merton, *Contemplative Prayer* (Garden City, NY: Doubleday, 1969), 42.

3. In Hebrews 13:15, we are told to "continually offer God a sacrifice of praise." We shouldn't be surprised when worship costs us something. What are you willing to sacrifice this week in order to worship God?

4. What are we to offer as our spiritual worship, according to Romans 12:1?

When we offer God ourselves—our bodies, our minds, our hearts, our dreams, our possessions, all that we love most—He considers it the supreme act of worship.

Quiet your heart and enjoy His presence. . . . He longs to pour blessings over you.

"Put me to the test, says the LORD of hosts, and see if I do not open the floodgates of heaven for you, and pour down upon you blessing without measure." (Malachi 3:10)

God will never be outdone in generosity. When we offer Him the sacrifice of worship, we should have a holy expectancy that what He'll give in return will be worth any price. God longs to open the floodgates of heaven for us, to pour down upon us blessing without measure. Don't let anything get in the way of this. Sin, noise, and busyness all can block the flow of these gifts. Take some time to examine your heart, looking for anything that God is asking you to remove so that there is room for Him to give you what you need.

Conclusion

"O come, bless the Lord, all you servants of the Lord, you who stand in the house of the Lord throughout the nights." (Psalm 134:1)

It may seem strange to worship throughout the night. This is an image of offering God the sacrifice of praise in the midst of the darkness of our sorrows, and it isn't an easy thing to do. Nevertheless, as Scottish minister George Matheson writes below, this is the time when our faith is perfectly tested:

> It is easy for me to worship in the summer sunshine… But when the songbirds cease and the fruit falls from the trees, will my heart continue to sing? Will I remain in God's house at night? Will I love Him simply for who He is? Am I willing to "keep watch for one hour" (Mark 14:37) with Him in His Gethsemane? Will I help Him carry His cross up the road of suffering to Calvary?…
>
> If I can do these things, then my worship is complete and my blessing glorious. Then I have indeed shown Him love during the time of His humiliation. My faith has seen Him in His lowest state, and yet my heart has recognized His majesty through His humble disguise. And at last I truly know that I desire not the gift but the Giver. Yes, when I can remain in His house through the darkness of night and worship Him, I have accepted Him for Himself alone.[8]

How can we turn away from the One who gave everything to save us? What cost could be too great? How can we allow distractions to get in the way of offering God the worship He is due? And isn't it just like Him, the Giver of all good things, to return with blessing upon blessing anything that we've lifted up to Him?

My Resolution

In what specific way will I apply what I learned in this lesson?

Examples:

1. I will "offer [my body] as a living sacrifice, holy and pleasing to God" (Romans 12:1) by setting my alarm and getting up fifteen minutes earlier than usual so I have time to sit in silence in God's presence.

2. I will try to "pray without ceasing" (1 Thessalonians 5:17) by choosing a time in the day that I normally spend in mindless thought (e.g. taking a shower, driving, preparing a meal) and talk to God as I do that activity.

---

[8] L. B. Cowman, *Streams in the Desert* (Grand Rapids, MI: Zondervan, 1997), 460.

3. I will spend an hour in adoration or go to Mass one time in addition to Sunday.

My Resolution:

Catechism Clips

CCC 1123 "The purpose of the sacraments is to sanctify men, to build up the Body of Christ and, finally, to give worship to God. Because they are signs they also instruct. They not only presuppose faith, but by words and objects they also nourish, strengthen, and express it. That is why they are called 'sacraments of *faith*.'"

CCC 1380 It is highly fitting that Christ should have wanted to remain present to his Church in this unique way. Since Christ was about to take his departure from his own in his visible form, he wanted to give us his sacramental presence; since he was about to offer himself on the cross to save us, he wanted us to have the memorial of the love with which he loved us "to the end," even to the giving of his life. In his Eucharistic presence he remains mysteriously in our midst as the one who loved us and gave himself up for us, and he remains under signs that express and communicate this love:

> The Church and the world have a great need for Eucharistic worship. Jesus awaits us in this sacrament of love. Let us not refuse the time to go to meet him in adoration, in contemplation full of faith, and open to making amends for the serious offenses and crimes of the world. Let our adoration never cease.

Verse Study

See Appendix 2 for instructions on how to complete a verse study.

John 4:24

1. Verse:

2. Paraphrase:

3. Questions:

4. Cross-references:

5. Personal Application:

Lesson 2
BALANCE IN YOUR SCHEDULE

Introduction

If I could truly have anything I wanted for my birthday, I would choose an extra twenty-four hours to use as I pleased. I fantasize about how much catching up I could do with this bonus time. And then I unwrap a new blender. Some women get irritated with gifts that have to do with cleaning or cooking. I don't. If it's a gift that's going to save me time, I say *bring it*. Throw a little chocolate in there and I'll be extra happy (I need the caffeine to keep me going).

I'm in the midst of a state of slight obsession over my calendar. For years, I've used an electronic calendar that supposedly is storing and updating all sorts of interesting facts about me in cyberspace. In theory, that means hackers could find out when I go to the dentist if they really wanted to. Except that in my case, the whole backup failed.

I woke up recently to something that I had fantasized about for years: My electronic calendar had nothing on it for the day. "How delightful!" I thought. "Twenty-four bonus hours!" But then I started feeling a little unsettled. I had a niggling sense that there was somewhere I was supposed to be. I looked ahead, and *all* the days as far as I could see were blank. I moved into full-blown panic when I realized that my calendar had been erased. I hurried to a computer expert, only to be told that I hadn't updated something essential, and as a result, my calendar hadn't been backed up. I've spent the past few weeks adjusting to my new normal. I meet each day with an awareness that I'm very likely not showing up for something or am forgetting someone's birthday. For a recovering perfectionist who really likes to follow through, it's pretty much a nightmare.

Because God never wastes any of our life experiences (it all can be redeemed by Him), I know that He is trying to teach me something. Maybe He's showing me the benefit of starting with a clean slate. (I'm not suggesting that you hit Delete on your online calendar or throw out your paper one, but don't you agree that sometimes we need a fresh start in our approach to our schedules?)

One thing is for sure—there's a better way to live than racing around from one appointment to another, worn out from the constant activity. All the things that we call "progress" seem to have sapped us of some much-needed white space. I know that God is calling us to a place of refreshment. And I want to go there. Not just for my next vacation; I want to go *now*. This is a place where every moment can be sacred. There's time for relationships. We can refuel there.

If you're starting this lesson feeling a little depleted and desperate for more hours in the day, you're in good company. If you're feeling empty, you've come to the right place.

I have no doubt that God's going to reveal some things to us this week that will give us hope. But be prepared—He doesn't magically create calm in the schedule. He asks us to be a part of the restoration. We'll need to cooperate in the journey toward balance in our schedules. But we aren't alone. We've got each other, and we've got Him. And that makes all the difference in the world.

Day One
STEWARDS, NOT OWNERS

1. According to Psalm 24:1, what belongs to God?

2. Where does everything we have come from? See Job 1:21 and James 1:17.

There is an enormous difference between being an owner and being a steward. Because owners' resources belong to them, it's fully within their right to use them as they please. By contrast, stewards have been placed in charge of something that belongs to someone else. Good stewards are always aware of how the owner would like his or her resources used, and then they use them accordingly. Decisions are based on what the owner would prefer, not what feels pleasant to the steward.

While the world tells us that we own all that we have, Scripture says that God is the real owner and we are the stewards. In 1 Corinthians 6:19–20, Saint Paul wrote, "Do you not know that . . . you are not your own? For you have been purchased at a price." That price was Christ's own life. He gave it in exchange for our freedom. Everything we have is an undeserved gift from Him. One of the most precious of those gifts that God has entrusted to us is time. We are to steward it well.

3. How is your view of your schedule impacted when you see yourself as a steward rather than as an owner of your time?

4. Jesus described a faithful steward in the following way: "Who then is the faithful and prudent steward whom his master will put in charge of his servants to distribute the food allowance at the proper time? Blessed is that servant whom his master on arrival finds doing so." (Luke 12:42–43) A good steward is the one whom God finds doing the things that matter to the master. Take a look at the upcoming week on your calendar. What things on your schedule matter most to God?

Quiet your heart and enjoy His presence. . . . You need Him as much as you need the air you breathe.

God is all about relationships. This is important to keep in mind, or we can make the mistake of assuming that as long as we're serving God, He's pleased with how we are spending our time. God doesn't just want us to pour our time into serving Him and others. He wants us to cultivate a relationship with Him, which means spending time with Him in prayer. You may wonder exactly how much time He wants us to spend with Him. The answer? As much time as it takes to maintain intimacy.

Spending time with God should be the primary goal of each day. There's no better time to do this than at the start of the day, because once we get going, distractions start to fill our minds. We head off into the day, having decided to handle things on our own without the game-changing help of God's grace. This may not be a conscious decision, but regardless, it's the decision we've made. God is a gentleman and won't force Himself into our schedules. We need to invite Him in.

For to you I will pray, LORD;
in the morning you will hear my voice;
In the morning I will plead before you and wait.

I rise before dawn and cry out;
I put my hope in your words. (Psalm 5:3–4; 119:147 NAB)

Day Two
THE BIG ROCKS

A time-management expert taught an important principle to a group of students, beginning by placing a gallon-sized mason jar on a table. He filled it to the brim with fist-sized rocks, and then asked the class, "Is this jar full?" They all agreed it was. He disagreed, and proceeded to pour gravel into the jar. The gravel settled into the spaces between the rocks, and he posed his question again: "Is this jar full?" A little less certain this time, the students said the jar *was* full now. Shaking his head, he poured sand into the jar. The sand found little crevices, and proved that the jar had still had room. "Is this jar full?" asked the man. The students felt it had to be—there wasn't any room left in the jar. Out came a pitcher of water, and it was added to the mixture in the jar. "What was the point of my illustration?" asked the expert.

An enthusiastic student said, "It makes the point that if we organize ourselves well and do the big things first, we can always fit in a little bit more!"

"No," said the time-management expert. "It means that if we don't put the big rocks in first, we'll never be able to fit them."

We all have limits. Every day, there will be things that we wish we could have done that are left unfinished. We can't always fit in a little bit more. A life well lived is made up of days when the things that are most important are done first and many good things remain undone. As Stephen R. Covey wisely wrote, "The key is not to prioritize what's on your schedule, but to schedule your priorities."[9]

---

[9] Stephen R. Covey, A. Roger Merrill, and Rebecca R. Merrill, *First Things First* (New York: Simon & Schuster, 1996), 161.

1. List your top three priorities in the space below. Look at your calendar. Are your priorities scheduled, or do you go through the day assuming you'll give time to them somehow?

2. Read Ephesians 5:15–20. What advice is given in this passage regarding the use of our time?

3. We run into difficulties when too many commitments in our lives feel like "big rocks." "It's *all* important!" we say. What insight do we gain from Ecclesiastes 3:1–8 regarding seasons of life and time management?

There are certain seasons of life that are more demanding than others. Everyone acknowledges that December is an especially busy time of year, and many consider May to be the new December, with the countless activities tied to school finishing for the summer. An accountant finds that the season directly preceding April 15 is taxing and demanding. A woman in med school is in a season of life when her focus on her studies likely demands all she's got. During each of these seasons, life will probably feel out of balance because an unusual amount of focus is being placed on one specific area. But as long as Christ remains at the center, things will come back into place with time. That season will pass. A time of greater balance will return. A wise woman won't rush the process. She will recognize that during that busy season, she'll have to say no to many good things in order to keep life from going off the rails. She'll have to practice patience as she puts other interests and demands on the back burner.

4. Are you attempting to do in your current season of life something that you sense God would like you to wait to experience in a later season?

Quiet your heart and enjoy His presence. . . . He is always there, right by your side.

Throughout Keeping In Balance, *a steady theme has been the importance of putting God first. He deserves to be our highest priority. This doesn't mean, however, that our relationship with God becomes a box that we tick on our to-do list. The spiritual dimension of our lives shouldn't be one more thing that we are attempting to manage in our schedule. Jesus should be found at the* center *of our lives, His presence and Spirit permeating everything we say and do. He's not just a part of our lives; He's at the helm and the heart of it all. We can talk to Him throughout the day, asking His advice, praying He'll give us the right words for a difficult conversation, thanking Him for an unexpected blessing. . . .*

When we find that we've spent hours without paying any attention to Him, all we have to do is inwardly turn back to Him. We can pray, "I'm so sorry that my mind has been so far away from you! Thank you for being there for me even when I'm not paying attention. Help me to tune in to you as I go forward." We can practice the constant presence of God in any season of life.

"The main thing about Christianity is not the work we do, but the relationship we maintain and the atmosphere produced by that relationship. That is all God asks us to look after, and it is the one thing that is being continually assailed." —Oswald Chambers, 1874–1917, Scottish Preacher

Day Three
MINUTE BY MINUTE

"A time is set for every affair and for every work." (Ecclesiastes 3:17)

"The wise heart knows times and judgments. Yes, there is a time and a judgment for everything." (Ecclesiastes 8:5–6)

1. Once we've got the big rocks of our priorities scheduled, we need to wisely schedule the sand and gravel tasks. The first step is to establish a plan. The next is execution. Both are equally important. Executing a plan requires a wise use of the minutes in the day. What methods of time management do you find most helpful? See Appendix 4, "Time Management Tips," for some additional ideas on how to better manage time.

2. For most of us, there is more expected of us than we can possibly get done in a day. Distractions come and can easily cause us to lose sight of what is most important. Dorothy Haskin, author of *A Practical Guide to Prayer*, wrote the following story of a concert violinist who was asked the secret of her mastery of the instrument:

> The woman answered the question with two words: "Planned neglect." Then she explained. "There were many things that used to demand my time. When I went to my room after breakfast, I made my bed, straightened the room, dusted, and did whatever seemed necessary. When I finished my work, I turned to my violin practice. That system prevented me from accomplishing what I should on the violin. So I reversed things. I deliberately planned to neglect everything else until my practice period was complete. And that program of planned neglect is the secret of my success."[10]

---

[10] Dorothy C. Haskin, *A Practical Guide to Prayer* (Chicago: Moody Press, 1951), 32.

What are the most common distractions in your life? How can you practice "planned neglect" in order to ensure you don't fritter away the minutes in the day?

3. When we find ourselves consistently running short on time, it's wise to analyze *why* we are doing certain activities. What is our motivation? Read the following quotes, and circle the one that you relate to the most.

> "I have too much on my plate. When I look at the motivation behind my behavior, I realize I'm doing many things because they are my personal goals. I want to accomplish them, no matter what it costs me or those around me."

> "I don't have time for all I need to do. But if I don't do these things, then I'll let people down, and they won't think as highly of me. I'm afraid to lose their respect."

> "I'm struggling to find time to do my job well. I just get so tired of all those tasks, and need to have a little fun! So I add fun stuff to my schedule, but then it all gets to be a little too much and I have trouble keeping it all together. But what am I supposed to do? Just work all the time?"

There is something each of these scenarios has in common: None of the motivations are grounded in doing what God desires. God cares how we steward our time, moment by moment.

Take a look at your calendar. Ask yourself why you are doing what you are doing. Do you see any activities that you are doing for the wrong reasons? If so, list them here.

Quiet your heart and enjoy His presence. . . . Invite Him into every moment of your day.

"You say grace before meals. All right. But I say grace before the concert and the opera, and grace before the play and pantomime, and grace before I open a book, and grace before sketching, painting, swimming, fencing, boxing, walking, playing, dancing and grace before I dip the pen in the ink." —
G. K. Chesterton

Every moment of our day is a gift from God, and He longs to infuse each one with His presence. We invite Him into the simplest of our tasks when we turn our hearts to Him in prayer. Every moment is made sacred when we live with an awareness that He is there and will faithfully stay close.

When we start our day with a period of focused prayer, we connect to God, gain His guidance for our schedule, and are filled with all we need to live as He calls us to. Throughout the day, we can shoot up "arrow prayers"—quick hellos, thank-yous, and pleas for help. We don't need to interrupt the task at hand to pray in this way. Because of this, every minute has the potential to be spent in prayer.

CCC 2659 We learn to pray at certain moments by hearing the Word of the Lord and sharing in his Paschal mystery, but his Spirit is offered us at all times, in the events of each day, to make prayer spring up from us. Jesus' teaching about praying to our Father is in the same vein as his teaching about providence: time is in the Father's hands; it is in the present that we encounter him, not yesterday nor tomorrow, but today: "O that today you would hearken to his voice! Harden not your hearts."

Day Four
THE HOLY SPIRIT'S HELP

Once we've made sure our priorities are on our calendar and have determined to make each minute in the day count, we often hit a barrier. *We don't feel like doing what we know is right.* Our will is powerful, and it can derail the best laid plans. Thankfully, God hasn't left us alone to battle our wills. He's placed the game-changing Holy Spirit into our hearts. The Holy Spirit gives strength to Christians, helping us to do what we should, even when we don't feel like it.

1. Who is the Holy Spirit? The Holy Spirit is not an impersonal force or a warm feeling. He is a divine person who has thoughts, emotions, and a will (Romans 15:30, Ephesians 4:30). He is the helper sent by God who advocates for us (John 15:26). He convicts us of sin (John 16:8), leads us (Romans 8:14), reveals truth to us (John 16:13), strengthens and encourages us (Acts 9:31), and comforts us (John

14:16). What additional things do you learn about the Holy Spirit from the following passages?

Romans 8:16

Romans 8:26

What do you need from the Holy Spirit today?

2. Read Ephesians 3:14–19 and answer the following questions.

   A. Where does the Holy Spirit dwell? (see verses 16-17)

   B. What does the Holy Spirit strengthen us with? (see verse 16)

   C. When we are rooted and grounded in love, what does God want us to have the strength to comprehend? (see verses 17–19)

It is a question of an inner strength which is rooted in love (cf. Ephesians 3:17), which St. Paul writes about to the faithful of Ephesus: may the Father 'grant you in accord with the riches of his glory to be strengthened with power through his Spirit in the inner self' (Ephesians 3:16). Paul prays to the Father to give this higher power to those to whom he is writing. Christian tradition lists this power among the 'gifts of the Holy Spirit,' deriving them from the text of Isaiah which lists them as the characteristics of the Messiah (cf. Isaiah 11:2). Among the gifts with which Christ's most holy soul is filled, the Holy Spirit also gives to Christ's followers the fortitude which he was champion of in his life and death. One can say that the Christian who is involved in the 'spiritual combat' has a share in the strength of the cross!

> The Spirit intervenes with a deep, continuing action at every moment and under all aspects of Christian life in order to guide human desires in the right direction, which is the direction of generous love of God and neighbor, following the example of Jesus. For this purpose the Holy Spirit strengthens the will, making the person capable of resisting temptations and of gaining victory in internal and external struggles. The Spirit enables the Christian to overcome the power of evil and especially Satan, like Jesus who was led by the Spirit into the desert (cf. Luke 4:1) and of fulfilling the demands of a life according to the Gospel.[11]

3. God wants to strengthen us through the power of the Holy Spirit. According to Psalm 32:3–5 and 66:18, what can get in the way of the Holy Spirit's work in our lives?

To confess means "to agree with." When the Holy Spirit reveals truth to us and the result is a feeling of conviction (we know something we did was wrong), we have a choice: We can agree with what He's revealed or run from the truth. When we confess our sin, we are agreeing with what the Holy Spirit has revealed. We're agreeing that the things we've done are sinful. That's the first step. The next is agreeing with the truth of God's forgiving nature. "If we acknowledge our sins, he is faithful and just and will forgive our sins and cleanse us from every wrongdoing." (1 John 1:9) After we have confessed our sin, God forgives. We need to believe and embrace that truth wholeheartedly.

Sometimes we mistake a feeling of condemnation for the convicting work of the Holy Spirit. The Holy Spirit does not condemn. "Now there is no condemnation for those who are in Christ Jesus." (Romans 8:1) Condemnation is the work of the enemy of our soul, who loves nothing more than making us feel dirty, worthless, judged, and unforgivable. This is the opposite of the way the Holy Spirit works. The Holy Spirit reveals truth to us, and immediately woos the merciful Father for our restoration.

---

[11] Saint John Paul II, "General Audience: The Spirit Gives Strength to Christians," June 26, 1991, http://www.vatican.va/holy_father/john_paul_ii/audiences/alpha/data/aud19910626en.html.

The Holy Spirit works in our hearts, reminding us that we are daughters of God. There is nothing we can do that's beyond the reach of God's mercy.

Quiet your heart and enjoy His presence. . . . May He strengthen you with power.

"If we live in the Spirit let us also follow the Spirit." (Galatians 5:25)

The Holy Spirit is living and active. This means that He can move with the ups and downs and ebb and flow of our lives. Even when we feel that we are running at breakneck speed, He can keep up. He's with us wherever we go. But we want to get to a place where we are letting the Holy Spirit set the pace. We want to follow the Spirit's lead, rather than just asking Him to bless us in what we think is best.

When we are keeping in step with the Spirit (instead of trying to run ahead of Him), we put our schedules under God's control. We ask Him to lead, guide, convict, strengthen, and help us. We give over control of our calendars, and He gives back all we need to experience true fullness of life.

Sometimes taming our schedules seems impossible. When we feel like that, we need to remember that with God, all things are possible (Luke 1:37). The Holy Spirit dwells in us, and fills us with hope. This hope assures us that the Holy Spirit can infuse us with the self-control we need to get a grip and make the changes that lead to peace-filled living.

The Holy Spirit is working in you, giving you the desire and the power to steward your time well. "For God is the one who, for his good purpose, works in you, both to desire and to work." (Philippians 2:13)

Day Five
MARGIN

The Holy Spirit is sometimes called the "gentle guest of our souls." One of the gifts that the Holy Spirit places within us is gentleness. God loves to see us draw on the Holy Spirit's gift of gentleness, which helps us to be kind to others even when our natural inclination is to be harsh. But God isn't only concerned about us treating *others* with gentleness. He wants us to treat *ourselves* gently. He sees us ruled by expectations, overload, and stress. We push ourselves as if we are limitless, but we are not. The Holy Spirit gives us the strength to do things we would have thought were impossible, but it's not for the purpose of our keeping an unhealthy schedule fueled by an inability to say no.

1. What were Jesus' instructions to the disciples after a period of demanding work and ministry? See Mark 6:30–32.

2. What does CCC 2184 have to say about the rhythm of human life? Is this rhythm reflected in your life?

If we're going to treat ourselves gently, we'll need to learn to live with margin.

> The conditions of modern-day living devour margin. If you are homeless, we send you to a shelter. If you are penniless, we offer you food stamps. If you are breathless, we connect you to oxygen. But if you are marginless, we give you yet one more thing to do.

> Marginless is being thirty minutes late to the doctor's office because you were twenty minutes late getting out of the bank because you were ten minutes late dropping the kids off at school because the car ran out of gas two blocks from the gas station—and you forgot your wallet.

> Margin, on the other hand, is having breath left at the top of the staircase, money left at the end of the month, and sanity left at the end of adolescence.[12]

Why are we so reluctant to carve out room for margin in our lives? How unhappy do we have to be with our schedules before we'll make choices that bring some relief? Part of the trouble lies in the fact that the pain caused by lack of margin isn't always manifested outwardly. It's something felt—an inner ache for something different or better. Because we can't always put our finger on the specific problem, we're slower to solve it.

---

[12] Richard A. Swenson, *Margin: Restoring Emotional, Physical, Financial, and Time Reserves to Overloaded Lives* (Colorado Springs: NavPress, 2004), 13.

3. In which area of your life are you feeling a lack of margin? (Think about your finances, relationships, time, physical health, emotional health. . . .)

4. What answer does Joshua 24:15 give to the excuse, "But I just can't say no"?

Quiet your heart and enjoy His presence. . . . Let's give Him the time He deserves.

If we say that we want our schedules to be under God's control instead of our own, we will have to carve out some margin. This is because what God wants from us is our availability. How many of us have schedules so tight that there's no time for relationships? God may have a divine appointment planned—a person He wants to place in our path for their benefit and ours—but we rush by, late to the next appointment. God wants us to be available to walk the second mile with someone in need (Matthew 5:41). He asks us to always be ready with an explanation for the hope within us (1 Peter 3:15). He wants us to carry one another's burdens (Galatians 6:2). The people God wants us to meet are often unexpected; these meetings can't be scheduled. We need margin on the calendar so that we can be available to God. The other option is to tune out the needs around us. But in doing so, do we tune out God?

Conclusion

There is no time like the present for change. Things are not going to get easier around the corner, because each season of life brings with it unique challenges.

The starting point for change must be taking some time to meditate on our identity in Christ. We are God's beloved daughters– not His work horses. Our worth is not found in what we achieve. It isn't measured by what people think of us. It doesn't increase with a pay raise or a nicer car. Our worth and security are rooted and grounded in God's unconditional love for us. When we have "the strength to comprehend . . . what is the breadth and length and height and depth [of that love, when we] know the love of Christ that surpasses knowledge, [we are] filled with all the fullness of God." (Ephesians 3:18–19) When we're filled with the fullness of God, we can rest. We can trust God with our schedules. We can be at peace.

The alternative is doing much of what we do for the wrong reasons. The result? Our fear of failure will skyrocket. Our weariness will increase. We'll feel trapped on a treadmill that's going nowhere.

Are you ready to step off the treadmill? Can you hand your calendar to the Lord and ask Him to order it as He wills? Will you lift your focus to heaven, recognizing that what matters here might not matter at all there?

> If you read history you will find that the Christians who did most for the present world were those who thought most of the next. The apostles themselves, who set out on foot to convert the Roman Empire, the great men who built up the Middle Ages, the English evangelicals who abolished the slave trade, all left their mark on earth, precisely because their minds were occupied with Heaven. It is since Christians have largely ceased to think of the other world that they have become so ineffective in this one. Aim at Heaven and you will get earth "thrown in." Aim at earth and you will get neither. —C. S. Lewis

My Resolution

In what specific way will I apply what I learned in this lesson?

Examples:

1. God has revealed some areas where I need to make some changes, but the truth is, I don't *want* to change. It's hard and uncomfortable. As a first step, I will pray every day that the Holy Spirit will help break down the resistance in my heart to what God is asking me to do. I will ask Him to help me want what He wants, how He wants it, when He wants it.

2. I will identify one area of my life where I would like to use my time more wisely. This might be an area where I am spending too much time, or an area that I've been neglecting and now need to focus on. I'll set a specific goal in this area, and work toward it every day.

3. I will find a friend who can hold me accountable for the specific goal I set for this week. I will give him or her permission to ask me how I'm doing and if I'm following through on my commitment.

My Resolution:

Catechism Clips

CCC 2184 Just as God "rested on the seventh day from all his work which he had done," human life has a rhythm of work and rest. The institution of the Lord's Day helps everyone enjoy adequate rest and leisure to cultivate their familial, cultural, social, and religious lives.

CCC 2659 We learn to pray at certain moments by hearing the Word of the Lord and sharing in his Paschal mystery, but his Spirit is offered us at all times, in the events of *each day*, to make prayer spring up from us. Jesus' teaching about praying to our Father is in the same vein as his teaching about providence: time is in the Father's hands; it is in the present that we encounter him, not yesterday nor tomorrow, but today: "O that *today* you would hearken to his voice! Harden not your hearts."

Verse Study

See Appendix 2 for instructions on how to complete a verse study.

Revelation 2:2–4

1. Verse:

2. Paraphrase:

3. Questions:

4. Cross-references:

5. Personal Application:

NOTES

Lesson 3

BALANCE THROUGH REST

Introduction

You know things are a little out of kilter when a concussion feels like a mini-vacation. My days had been filled to the brim with Christmas preparations, family dynamics, writing deadlines, and an impending move to a new state. I had been experiencing an underlying sense that I was skating close to my limit, but I couldn't see any option but to keep going. And then God stopped me in my tracks. As I walked through a doorway that required ducking my head, I got distracted and walked hard into the doorframe. I hit it with enough force to land backward on the floor, stunned that I'd been too preoccupied to lower my head. Dizziness and nausea sent me to bed, and once I got there, I decided it felt pretty nice—rest; no one expecting anything of me; guilt-free relaxation.

Just for the record, this is not the way God wants us to pursue rest. God created us with a need to slow down. He knows we weren't meant to keep going at a nonstop, frantic pace. He's very familiar with our limits. Knowing that the pull to achieve and acquire would always be strong, He gave us an oasis in the midst of the rat race. That place to stop and refuel is called the Sabbath.

Just saying the word *Sabbath* can sound weird to us. It's a religious word, one seldom heard in our fast-paced culture. Saying, "I'm celebrating the Sabbath tomorrow," causes most listeners to raise an eyebrow and look for the nearest exit to get away from the freaky religious talk. And be assured, incorporating a Sabbath rhythm into our lives is countercultural.

But where is our culture leading us? Do we like where we're going? Are we enjoying the journey? Or is it possible that in our ceaseless busyness we are bypassing real life?

If you are tired, if you are weary, then I pray this lesson leaves you with the following truths planted firmly in your heart:

You have permission to rest.
God commands you to rest.
The rhythm God set up for rest is the Sabbath.

You weren't made to work so long and hard. God offers you rest. Invite Him in to overcome the overload in your life.

Day One
THE FREEDOM OF REST

The book of Exodus is the story of God teaching His people how to be free after He rescued them from slavery in Egypt. For hundreds of years in Egypt, the Israelites had been forced to work without stopping. Their value was based entirely on their productivity. When God led them to the Promised Land, He began to teach them that their value wasn't based on what they produced; it was rooted in their identity as God's beloved children.

God gave the Israelites the Ten Commandments to help them learn to walk in freedom. These rules were intended to clarify which choices would lead them back to captivity and which would help them experience the liberty of being God's children.

One way God taught them how to walk in freedom was to insist that they not let anything be more important to them than He. This was the first commandment: "I am the LORD your God, who brought you out of the land of Egypt, out of the house of slavery. You shall not have other gods beside me. You shall not make for yourself an idol." (Exodus 20:2–4) Making God the highest priority in their lives would help them to follow all the other commandments.

1. What did God command in Deuteronomy 5:12–15? Why might this help teach the Israelites that their worth was to be found in Him, not in what they produced?

"The Jews' insistence on keeping their laws, especially the Sabbath law, has irritated despots and dictators down through history. Slave masters, whether ancient or modern, know that people who feel free to take one day out of seven to rest and pray, are people that are truly free the other six days of the week."[13] —Susan K. Rowland

2. Do you see any parallels between the Israelites' life of slavery in Egypt and our lives today?

3. The Ten Commandments weren't only for the Old Testament Israelites; we're to obey them, too. It's interesting that the Sabbath commandment[14] is the only one that has to do with how we are to care for ourselves. And it's interesting how quickly we ignore it. A well-known philosopher and physician, Albert Schweitzer, said, "Do not let Sunday be taken from you. If your soul has no Sunday, it becomes an orphan." Do you agree or disagree with this statement? Share your thoughts below.

4. What is your current experience of the Sabbath? What do you think we lost when Sunday became a day just like every other day of the week? Are you feeling the effects of a fast-paced life with no time to rest?

Quiet your heart and enjoy His presence. . . . Take time to exhale.

"Sabbath is the time set aside for my soul to breathe . . . really breathe. So much of my daily life is inhaling, inhaling, inhaling—taking so much in and holding my breath hoping I can manage it all. But we can't just inhale. We must also exhale—letting it all out before God and establishing a healthier rhythm by which to live." [15] *—Lysa TerKeurst*

---

[13] Susan K. Rowland, "Sabbath Moments in a Busy World," AmericanCatholic.org, http://www.americancatholic.org/Newsletters/CU/preview.aspx?id=256.

[14] "Remember the Sabbath day—keep it holy, six days you may labor and do all your work, but the seventh day is a Sabbath of the LORD your God. You shall not do any work." (Exodus 20:8–10)

[15] Lysa TerKeurst, *Unglued: Making Wise Choices in the Midst of Raw Emotions* (Grand Rapids, MI: Zondervan, 2012), 153.

Take a moment and pay attention to your breathing. Slow down by inhaling for ten seconds and slowly exhaling for ten seconds. Do this three times, to help your mind and body to settle. Take some time now to talk to God about the way you usually spend Sunday. Is He calling you to rest? Talk to Him about the barriers that prevent you from stopping your work. Ask Him to help you walk in freedom as His daughter—one valued because of who she is, not what she does.

Day Two
LETTING GOD SET THE PACE

How often do we tell each other, "I'm so busy," as if it's a badge of honor? But if we're trying to become more and more like Christ, we'll see the benefit of following an inner rhythm different from the constant busyness that our culture lauds.

1. Read and describe the scene in Mark 1:32–34. What were the people's needs? What did they probably hope for and expect from Jesus the morning after these events?

2. What did Jesus do the morning after the events of Mark 1:32–34, and how did the people react? See Mark 1:35–37.

The people wanted more of Jesus, but His actions weren't determined by people's expectations or needs. He didn't wait until every person had been helped, He didn't tell the disciples where He was going, and He didn't check to see if everyone was OK with Him taking a break. When it became clear that He needed rest and prayer, He knew that meant it was time to stop healing and teaching.

Jesus had an inner rhythm of work and rest that probably didn't make sense to the people around Him. That didn't deter Him, because He had predetermined to do whatever the Father told Him to do. Jesus explained this with the words, "I do not seek my own will but the will of the one who sent me." (John 5:30)

3. If anyone had an excuse to not stop, it was Jesus. List reasons why it would have made sense for Jesus to continually heal and teach during His time on earth.

It's hard for us to stop, pull back, and pray. What are the reasons you give when you say you are unable to pull back and rest? What gets in the way of your ability to celebrate the Sabbath?

As acutely as we feel the pressure to keep working without rest, most of our excuses seem a little feeble when they are compared with the reasons Jesus could have worked without ceasing. Yet Jesus knew the importance of pulling back and resting. If prayer and rest were so important to Jesus, shouldn't they be an important priority for us? Shouldn't they be a nonnegotiable part of our schedules?

4. Read Exodus 20:8–11. What reason was given in verse 11 for the keeping of the Sabbath?

"Just as God 'rested on the seventh day from all his work which he had done,' human life has a rhythm of work and rest. The institution of the Lord's Day helps everyone enjoy adequate rest and leisure to cultivate their familial, cultural, social and religious lives." (CCC 2184)

Quiet your heart and enjoy His presence. . . . He's waiting for you.

There's a beautiful aspect of the Sabbath that author Wayne Muller describes in his book Sabbath: Finding Rest, Renewal, and Delight in Our Busy Lives*:*

> *God creates the world in six days, and on the seventh day, God rests. But a closer reading of Genesis reveals that the Sabbath was not simply a day off. It says, "On the seventh day God finished God's work." How can this be? Wasn't the seventh day when God, exhausted, took time off and rested, satisfied with the laborious work of creation?*
>
> *The ancient rabbis teach that on the seventh day, God created menuha—tranquillity, serenity, peace, and repose—rest, in the deepest possible sense of fertile, healing stillness. Until the Sabbath, creation was unfinished. Only after the birth of menuha, only with tranquillity and rest, was the circle of creation made full and complete.*[16]

Beginning the week from this place of rest allows us to look ahead with a fresh perspective. Thank God for creating tranquility, serenity, peace, and repose. Think about how the creation of these things reveals His love for you. You are not His workhorse. You are His beloved. Come away with Him to a still place to find rest for your soul.

Day Three
TIME TO "BECOME"

"To Jews, Sabbath is not merely a day to rest, it is a day to become, to put aside all our doing for one day a week. That is why there are so many laws governing the Sabbath. In order to become who we are, we must stop doing what we normally do."[17] —Susan K. Rowland

1. What does Matthew 18:3 say we should become? In what way would resting on a Sabbath day help you to do that?

---

[16] Wayne Muller, *Sabbath: Finding Rest, Renewal, and Delight in Our Busy Lives* (New York: Bantam Books, 1999), 37.
[17] Rowland, "Sabbath Moments in a Busy World."

2. You do not need to experience illness or emotional collapse in order to have permission to take a rest. God has programmed it into your week, and asks you to "Come to me . . . and I will give you rest." (Matthew 11:28) God wants you to have time for the things that bring you joy and delight. List the activities and people that you enjoy and feel energized by.

The activities and people you listed in question 2 help form who you are. Take the time to experience wholeness by building your version of "play" into your week. What is a delight? What pours into you? What makes you feel that you have lost track of time? All of these are perfect activities for the Sabbath.

"On Sundays and other holy days of obligation, the faithful are to refrain from engaging in work or activities that hinder the worship owed to God, *the joy proper to the Lord's Day* [emphasis mine], the performance of the works of mercy, and the appropriate relaxation of mind and body." (CCC 2185) What brings you joy? Make time for it on the Sabbath.

3. In Matthew 19:19, Jesus tells us that we should love our neighbor as ourselves. How loved would your neighbor feel if you treated him or her the way you treat yourself? Do you need to grow in the area of self-care? Has lack of time prevented you from caring for your own needs? How could you use the Sabbath to become healthier?

4. As we saw in Lesson 1: Balance Through Worship, what is the most effective way for us to become the best women we can be, growing more and more like Christ? See 2 Corinthians 3:18.

Quiet your heart and enjoy His presence. . . . This is where you become the woman God is calling you to be.

In his sermon "On the Pure Love of God," Saint Augustine asked a probing question:

> *Suppose God proposed to you a deal and said, "I will give you anything you want. You can possess the whole world. Nothing will be impossible for you. . . . Nothing will be a sin, nothing forbidden. You will never die, never have pain, never have anything you do not want and always have anything you do want—except for just one thing: you will never see my face."*

> *Did a chill rise in your hearts, when you heard the words, "You will never see my face"? That chill is the most precious thing in you; that is the pure love of God.*

Let your love of God draw you to Him. Rest in His presence. As you behold His glory, you'll be transformed, becoming more like Him.

Day Four
TIME TO APPRECIATE WHAT YOU ALREADY HAVE

Sabbath is a time to stop, to refrain from being seduced by our desires. To stop working, stop making money, stop spending money. See what you have. Look around. Listen to your life. Do you really need more than this? Spend a day with your family. Instead of buying the new coffee maker, make coffee in the old one… hang out—do what they do in the picture without paying for it. Just stop. That is, after all, what they are selling in the picture: people who have stopped. You cannot buy stopped. You simply have to stop.[18] —Wayne Muller

---

[18] Muller, 137.

1. What happens when our desires go unchecked? See Exodus 20:17 and James 14-15.

2. So many of us feel driven to keep achieving and acquiring. When something is accomplished, it seems the bar has simply moved and we have a new set of goals to shoot for. Sometimes we feel like it's a fight just to keep our heads above water. Stop working? Stop making money? Stop striving? It sounds impossible. But God speaks into our harried lives with the words of Exodus 14:14, giving a different perspective. How do those words comfort or challenge you today?

3. Read 1 Timothy 6:7–9. Reflect on your own level of contentment. List below desires that are robbing you of being satisfied with what God has given you. Can you offer these desires back to God, trusting that if they are for your good, He will fight for them to be fulfilled? If so, write a short prayer to Him expressing those thoughts.

4. In her book *One Thousand Gifts*, Ann Voskamp reflects on a pastor's greatest life regret:

   Being in a hurry. Getting to the next thing without fully entering the thing in front of me. I cannot think of a single advantage I've ever gained from being in a hurry. But a thousand broken and missed things, tens of thousands, lie in the wake of all the rushing. . . . Through all that haste I thought I was *making up time*. It turns out I was *throwing it away*."[19]

[19] Ann Voskamp, *One Thousand Gifts: A Dare to Live Fully Right Where You Are* (Grand Rapids, MI: Zondervan, 2010), 65–6.

Take some time to reflect on these words. Begin a list below of the things you might be missing. Make a separate list of the things that you already have but often fail to appreciate.

Quiet your heart and enjoy His presence. . . . Take time to reflect on what you already have.

After God created the world, He rested on the seventh day. He delighted in everything that He'd made and said it was "very good." We can imitate God by delighting in what we've been given. Of course, we should do this every day, but it's an important component of taking a break on the Sabbath.

Seek the grace in the moment. Look for the simplest things that can bring you joy: A scented candle. The warm water in the shower. The delight of a child's smile. The softness of a blanket. LOOK. What blessings are surrounding you right now?

Day Five
TIME TO THINK

1. Do you find you often have to make decisions on the fly, without having time to think through the pros and cons thoroughly? Share an experience in which you made a hasty decision and later regretted the consequences. Would you have made a different decision if you'd taken time in solitude to think about it deeply, or asked someone you respected for advice?

2. Author Wayne Muller describes the effect lack of rest has on our decision making: "Without rest, we respond from a survival mode, where everything we meet assumes a terrifying prominence. When we are driving a motorcycle at high speed, even a small stone in the road can be a deadly threat. So, when we are moving faster and faster, every encounter, every detail inflates in importance, everything

seems more urgent than it really is, and we react with sloppy desperation."[20] Does this ring true to you? Why or why not?

3. When we stop and rest, we create a sacred space where we can meet with God. What do the following verses promise if we take the time to call out to Him in prayer? See Jeremiah 33:3, Proverbs 3:5–6, and James 1:5.

4. Our busy lives can make it hard to spend time with friends. This can result in loneliness, and it also means that we often make decisions alone. What insight does Proverbs 15:22 give regarding the importance of taking time to seek wise advice? Would freeing up your Sunday to celebrate the Sabbath create time to get together with friends whose counsel would help you grow in wisdom?

Quiet your heart and enjoy His presence. . . . See your choices from God's perspective.

God is all ready to show us the compass points that will lead us in the right direction. But too often, we go flying by without consulting Him. He also brings wise people into our lives, but it's only if we spend time with them that we'll benefit from it. If we protect the Sabbath as a day for communion— communion with our own thoughts, with God, and with loved ones—our decisions will be better.

Are you facing a decision now? Is there a situation that is troubling you? The Sabbath provides a wonderful opportunity to set aside time for deeper thought and prayer. But even now, you can take a "Sabbath moment" to prayerfully look at your motives. Ask God to purify them. Has He already revealed truths to you that are relevant to this situation? Ask the Holy Spirit to bring them to mind. Do you have God's perspective on the situation? Ask Him to help you see things in light of eternity.

---

[20] Muller, 5.

Conclusion

What did we lose when Sunday became a day just like every other day of the week? As Saint John Paul II said, "When Sunday loses its fundamental meaning and becomes merely a part of a 'weekend,' people stay locked within a horizon so limited that they can no longer see 'the heavens.'"

Friends, we have got to learn how to live according to the rhythm we were created for. Our bodies are crying out for rest. Our relationships are longing for greater depth. Our emotions need a sabbatical.

Ignoring the Sabbath is disobedience of God. That may sound extreme, but it's true. And the quality of our lives is in danger if we continue to neglect the third commandment. We are living wrong when all we want is for something to take the edge off, to help us disengage from our current reality. It's watching the clock for that point in the day when we can have a glass of wine to anesthetize our emotions. It's equating rest with coveting someone else's life through social media. It's filling our minds and feasting our eyes on things that we don't have but we want on the Internet. That isn't really living. That's living numb.

Could it be that in being able to check more things off the to-do list, we lose something more important—time to take a walk with a friend, bringing that relationship to a deeper place?

Could it be that in being able to make more money by working more hours or sealing the big deal, we lose something more important—time to refresh our souls and hear God's guiding, comforting voice?

There's so much to lose, yet so much to gain if we obey God and accept His offer of rest. When we slow down, we can delight in the people whom God places in our paths. We'll be able to look at people—really look at them—and try to imagine who they truly are. What might their dreams be? Their hopes? Their hurts? Exhale and see.

Of course, the most important component of the Sabbath is turning our focus toward God, and this is what will bring the greatest refreshment. Celebrating the Sabbath on Sunday makes sense, as we have the opportunity to go to Mass. In order to most enjoy our time with the Lord, we should keep a spiritual focus on the Sabbath. What are some ways we can do this? It's no coincidence that most parishes offer the sacrament of confession on Saturday. That is an excellent way to prepare for time with God on Sunday. We can make time to pray before Mass, asking Him to speak to our hearts in a special way as we receive Him in the Eucharist. We might choose to take a walk and thank God for His beautiful creation. We can try to keep an ongoing dialogue with Him during the day. We can choose to read Scripture before we fall asleep. We'll be most refreshed if we spend our Sabbath day not just relaxing, but remembering that God is always beside us, enjoying the day and our presence.

But none of this will happen unless we plan ahead. Celebrating the Sabbath begins the day before. No, it actually begins right now. It begins with a choice. Do you want more? Do you want to experience the life of balance that God created you for? The ball is in your court. You'll make time for what you consider most important.

"Come to me . . . and I will give you rest." (Matthew 11:28)

My Resolution

In what specific way will I apply what I learned in this lesson?

Examples:

1. I'll designate two boxes as my Sabbath boxes. One box will contain things that delight me. Happy projects I don't have time for during the week will be in this box. On the Sabbath, the box will come down and I'll be able to enjoy them. The other box is for things that drain me. Things that I need to fast from, like my phone, my computer, or my calendar, will go in that box for the duration of the day.

2. I'll build grocery shopping into my schedule on Saturday so that there's food in the house for Sunday and Monday morning. I'll think ahead to the clothes that I need for Monday morning, and make sure they are laundered and ready to go on Saturday.

3. I'll go to confession on Saturday in order to be spiritually prepared for a day of rest in God's presence on Sunday.

My Resolution:

Catechism Clips

CCC 2184 Just as God "rested on the seventh day from all his work which he had done," human life has a rhythm of work and rest. The institution of the Lord's Day helps everyone enjoy adequate rest and leisure to cultivate their familial, cultural, social and religious lives.

CCC 2185 On Sundays and other holy days of obligation, the faithful are to refrain from engaging in work or activities that hinder the worship owed to God, the joy proper to the Lord's Day, the performance of the works of mercy, and the appropriate relaxation of mind and body. Family needs or important social service can legitimately excuse from the obligation of Sunday rest. The faithful should see to it that legitimate excuses do not lead to habits prejudicial to religion, family life, and health.

Verse Study

See Appendix 2 for instructions on how to complete a verse study.

Isaiah 58:13-14

1. Verse:

2. Paraphrase:

3. Questions:

4. Cross-references:

5. Personal Application:

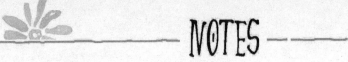

NOTES

Lesson 4

BALANCE THROUGH SIMPLICITY

Introduction

When I think of simplicity, I imagine breathing deeply, laughing until I cry, clean surfaces, time to wander, fresh laundry blowing in the wind, and really looking into people's eyes when I'm talking to them. What does simplicity mean to you? Less stuff? Less pressure? Less baggage? Less mess?

We live in a time when simplicity seems elusive. Even when we agree that less is more, we feel overwhelmed at the thought of paring down. Simplifying takes time, and our schedules are one of the many things that need to be simpler. Two dear friends of mine and I got together last summer, determined that we were going to simplify our lives. We committed to the journey together. Our first step was to simplify our possessions. We decided to have a garage sale and planned to give the money we collected to people in need. We started to gather things we wanted to sell, but then didn't have time to organize or price them. Now we're trying to shove it all back into the drawer or closet or storage room.

How can we hear God over the noise? How can we find Him through the clutter? How can we grow in intimacy with a God we can't see with our eyes when we're having trouble staying close to the people within reach? Could it be that we don't have much room for God because we're so full of everything else?

Have we bought into the American dream that true happiness comes from pursuing prosperity and success—and that it is our right? Are we so full of comfort, self-focus, and stuff (the buying of it, the taking care of it, and then the updating of it) that there is no room, no sacred space to behold God's greatness and glory? So we keep Him small so He fits into the little compartment in our lives that we've allocated to Him, and we head into the rat race.

Before we give up and assume that simplicity is never going to be possible for us, let's remember who is in control. We read in Acts 17:26 that when God made us, He determined the times set for us and the exact places where we would live. When and where we live is no mistake. And why did God pick this particular time in history and this place geographically for each one of us? We find the answer in Acts 17:27. He tailor-made each of our circumstances, "so that [we] might seek God, even perhaps grope for him and find him, though indeed he is not far from any one of us."

If all of this is a part of God's plan, then we can take heart. We can find hope. God knows what we're up against. He never asks anything of us that He doesn't equip us to accomplish.

God doesn't want us to simplify our lives so they are empty and boring. He wants us to clear space so that we can know Him more. Not only that, He wants us to *enjoy* Him. There is so much in creation and so much He puts in our days just to delight us. If we're rushing around, we're going to miss it.

Are you sick of the excess? Are you tired of being full of the things that ultimately don't satisfy? Are you ready to experience the *more* that God created you for? Are you hungry for God? Maybe even desperate for Him?

A simplified life leaves room for joy. There's time to be gentle. There's margin. There's sacred space for God.

Let's begin to clear the clutter so we can discover the pleasures that God has in store. A simplified life, a magnified God. Less of me, and more of Him.

"All external manifestations of the Christian life require internal foundations, and simplicity is no different." [21]

Day One and Day Two will focus our attention on two things required if we're going to pursue simplicity with a strong internal foundation. We'll first look at where we go to satisfy our hungry souls, then where we should place our focus on a daily basis. Days Three to Five will deal with specific problem zones in which we struggle to simplify.

---

[21] Richard A. Swenson, *Margin: Restoring Emotional, Physical, Financial, and Time Reserves to Overloaded Lives* (Colorado Springs: NavPress, 1992), 204.

Day One
THE SIMPLICITY OF LETTING GOD SATISFY OUR HUNGER

The book of Exodus introduces us to Moses, an Old Testament prophet, chosen by God to lead the Israelites out of slavery in Egypt. When we meet him in Exodus 33, we find a man who is longing for more of God.

1. How would you describe Moses' experience of the presence of God? See Exodus 33:11.

2. Moses wanted more of God when he was already experiencing quite a lot. When he met with God, Moses would enter the tent of meeting, and a cloud would come down and hover at the entrance to the tent, offering total intimacy for the two of them. But Moses wanted *more*. Describe his request in Exodus 33:18.

3. Moses was hungry, desperate for God. Are you? Or are you saturated with what our culture feeds us? We're surrounded by materialism (the glory of stuff), hedonism (the glory of pleasure), and individualism (the glory of self). Do you feel these things clamoring to get into your soul?

4. When God saw Moses' hunger for Him, He chose to grant his request. How did God say He would show Moses His glory? See Exodus 33:19—23.

God then told Moses to cut two stone tablets so that God could write on them. The next day, when God would reveal His glory to Moses, He would also write the Ten Commandments on those stones. This was round two; the first set of tablets had been broken when Moses saw that the Israelites had worshipped the golden calf in his absence. Moses did what God said and cut the two tablets.

The next day, when God passed before Moses, He revealed His glory by saying, "The LORD, the LORD, a God gracious and merciful, slow to anger and abounding in love and fidelity, continuing his love for a thousand generations." (Exodus 34:6–7) He displayed His holiness, His character, to Moses, who immediately knelt and bowed down before God, begging Him to stay with the Israelites, despite their constant tendency to turn away from Him.

Quiet your heart and enjoy His presence. . . . Let His grace, mercy, love, and faithfulness surround you.

God promised to remain faithful to His people, and with the Ten Commandments, laid out the guidelines that would help His people remain faithful to Him. In essence, God was saying, "There isn't room for both me and any other god. You're going to have to choose Me and reject what the people around you say matters more."

This is His message to us today. If we're going to move toward simplicity, we're going to have to get rid of some baggage that's cluttering our souls. What needs to go? What has a hold on your heart? The glory of stuff? The glory of pleasure? The glory of self? Ask God to help you to let it go. Ask Him to fill the empty space left behind with His own glorious and holy presence.

"Blessed are they who hunger and thirst for righteousness, for they will be satisfied." (Matthew 5:6)

Day Two
THE SIMPLICITY OF LESS SELF-FOCUS

1. Moses remained with the Lord for forty days without eating or drinking. Something interesting was observed when Moses returned to the Israelites, the two tablets in hand. What was it? See Exodus 34:29.

The Hebrew word for *radiant* is *qaran* (kaw-ran), which means "to send out rays like horns." Can you picture what he looked like? It must have looked absolutely amazing—especially to people who weren't desensitized by the special effects we see in film and on television. Why was his face shining? The glory that Moses had seen was so powerful that it literally lit him up.

But the most amazing thing of all is that Moses had no idea that his face was shining. He was glowing in the dark, yet was totally unaware of it! He was so focused on God and amazed by what had just been revealed to him that he wasn't paying any attention to himself.

This is a mark of true holiness. This is where we want to get to. No matter how much God might be working through us or allowing us to see or do wonderful things, we want to be focused on *Him*, not on what we look like. Anytime we are aware of our shining faces, or concerned about whether or not others are seeing our shining faces, our focus is in the wrong place.

2. How can we strike the balance of having a healthy self-image while resisting the temptation to be excessively self-focused? Give this some thought before looking up the following Bible verses. It's an important question to wrestle with. See 1 Corinthians 10:24, 2 Corinthians 5:15, and 2 Corinthians 10:12.

When we're trying so hard to present a "shining face" wherever we go, life gets complicated and exhausting. When we compare ourselves to others, we head down a path toward either pride or discouragement. Both tie our souls in knots.

When we come to the place of freedom where we don't even know whether our faces are shining or not, we start to taste simplicity. We're not worried about protecting our reputations or putting our best feet forward. Our eyes are fixed on Christ. How people respond to the way we live for Him is between them and God. We don't have to mentally go there. Life becomes simpler as we let go of striving to measure up. We start to realize that living to please Christ alone is true simplicity and freedom.

3. How is a lack of self-focus described in Matthew 16:24–25?

What does it mean to deny ourselves? Does it mean that who we are (our personalities, interests, gifts, unique qualities) doesn't matter and should be squelched? No. God created us, and delights in who we are. But it does mean that we take our eyes off ourselves and put them on others. We let go of the need to be right, the need to be understood, the need to be comfortable, the need to have every craving satisfied.

When we do this, we find that we can become content even when our circumstances aren't ideal. We depend on God, and find that He is utterly trustworthy. This is done on a moment-by-moment basis. Each moment, we try to become conscious of what we are focusing on. Are we motivated by our own wants, or are we seeking to please God and do what He wants? Some call this "dying to self." There's no better time to begin than right now. Each day, look for an opportunity to die to self. It could be not becoming defensive when someone questions you. Or saying no to some material comfort so that another person can be blessed. Or passing up an evening glass of wine so that you feel fresher in the morning, and more able to get up early to pray. What dying to self looks like in each of our lives will be unique. The important thing is to take the first step, "for whoever loses [her] life for [Christ's] sake will find it." (Matthew 16:25)

Quiet your heart and enjoy His presence. . . . Behold His glory.

When we behold God's glory, something amazing happens. The Holy Spirit works on us on the soul level, and transforms us so that we become more like Christ.

It cost Jesus everything for us to be able to gaze freely on God's glory. He wants nothing more than to see us transformed. But is this what we are experiencing? Are we experiencing the transforming power of the Holy Spirit at work within us?

In order to behold God's glory, we have to let go of our own. And this, my friend, is hard to do. This is radical living. It involves abandoning all sorts of behaviors that we are quite comfortable with.

We're comfortable with them in part because we are encouraged to live the American dream. We're commended for achievement, self-sufficiency, accumulation of possessions, productivity, and success in the here and now. And as we pursue these things, we feel emptier and emptier.

If we want to behold God's glory and there's no room—no sacred space for Him—if we're keeping Him small in our lives, there's just one solution: less of me and more of God.

What does less of me and more of God mean in your life? It will look different for each one of you. Take some time to sit in the presence of your loving heavenly Father, and ask Him to reveal to you how you can be freed from self-focus, and really experience life as it was intended to be lived.

Day Three
LESS STUFF

In our pursuit of simplicity, it's fair to say that we're up against a challenge. We live in a culture that consumes at a jaw-dropping rate. Consider the following statistics:

> The average person living in the United States uses 300 shopping bags worth of raw materials every week—weighing as much as a large luxury car. We would need the resources of three planets for everyone on Earth to live as people in the United States do.[22] (World Resources Institute, Center for a New American Dream)

> We are targeted by over 1,500 commercial messages a day, up from 560 per day in the 1960s. Advertisers are increasingly targeting young people. Companies spend more than $200 billion on advertising in the U.S. each year (and $435 billion worldwide). Less than $50 billion a year could provide adequate food, clean water, and basic education for the world's poorest. People around the world spend much more than this amount on makeup, perfumes, pet food, ocean cruises, and ice cream.[23](Center for a New American Dream, Worldwatch Institute)

Real simplicity will restore us, but it'll require swimming upstream.

---

[22] "Fast Facts About Consumption," Facing the Future, http://www.facingthefuture.org/ServiceLearning/FastFactsQuickActions/Consumption/tabid/176/Default.aspx#.UmpD3RYyxno.
[23] Ibid.

Read Luke 12:13–21.

1. When someone in the crowd brought a problem to Jesus, how did Jesus respond?

When we bring problems to Jesus, He often responds to us in the same way. He draws attention to the issues in our hearts, and challenges us to explore our motives and our need to change. We're usually looking for a quick fix, but God is more interested in our steady growth and transformation. When we're longing for a simpler life, we might call out to God in prayer, asking Him to relieve the stress. Sometimes He does, but more often, He asks us to look within and explore why we continue to make decisions that get in the way of our pursuit of simplicity. The problem isn't "out there." It's in our hearts.

> *CCC 1723* The beatitude we are promised confronts us with decisive moral choices. It invites us to purify our hearts of bad instincts and to seek the love of God above all else. It teaches us that true happiness is not found in riches or well-being, in human fame or power, or in any human achievement (however beneficial it may be) such as science, technology, or art, or indeed in any creature, but in God alone, the source of every good and of all love:
>
> All bow down before wealth. Wealth is that to which the multitude of men pay an instinctive homage. They measure happiness by wealth; and by wealth they measure respectability. . . . It is a homage resulting from a profound faith . . . that with wealth he may do all things. Wealth is one idol of the day and notoriety is a second. . . . Notoriety, or the making of a noise in the world—it may be called "newspaper fame"—has come to be considered a great good in itself, and a ground of veneration.[24]

2. While it was wise for the rich man to financially plan for his life before death, what did he fail to do?

---

[24] *Catechism of the Catholic Church*, 2nd ed. (Vatican City: Libreria Editrice Vaticana), #1723.

3. Do you see any parallels between the rich man's building of barns and the amount of time we put into caring for and updating our possessions?

4. What do you believe causes us to consume at such an alarming rate? Why are we able to justify buying luxuries when others lack basic necessities?

Quiet your heart and enjoy His presence. . . . You are fully known and loved.

Meditate on the following excerpt from Jen Hatmaker's book 7, *and respond to God in prayer. Ask Him if He's calling you to have a different attitude toward your possessions, and how that attitude should translate into action.*

A child says "me." An adult says "us." Maturity deciphers need from want, wisdom from foolishness. Growing up means curbing appetites, shifting from "me" to "we," understanding private choices have social consequences and public outcomes. Let's be consumers who silence the screaming voice that yells, "I WANT!" and instead listens to the quiet "we need," the marginalized voice of the worldwide community we belong to.[25]

"When I was a child, I used to talk as a child, think as a child, reason as a child; when I became a man, I put aside childish things. At present we see indistinctly, as in a mirror, but then face to face. At present I know partially; then I shall know fully, as I am fully known." *(1 Corinthians 13:11–12)*

---

[25] Jen Hatmaker, *7: An Experimental Mutiny Against Excess* (Nashville, TN: B&H Publishing Group, 2012), 94.

Day Four
LESS WASTE

"We received this world as an inheritance from past generations, but also as a loan from future generations, to whom we will have to return it!"[26]—Pope Francis

1. According to Psalm 24:1–2, whom do the earth's resources belong to? How should that affect our use of them?

2. When God gave mankind the responsibility of subduing the earth in Genesis 1:28, was that permission to use it in any way that we saw fit? See CCC 373.

3. Do you think that our use of the earth's resources is as much a spiritual issue as an environmental one? Why or why not?

While there are certainly important environmental issues at stake, the way we waste the earth's resources can also point to a spiritual issue within us. When we thoughtlessly waste, we are showing a lack of concern for those who will come after us. Like it or not, that's basic selfishness. Our motives aren't necessarily bad—we're just busy doing other things and it takes more time to be environmentally friendly. For example, it takes two seconds to throw away a used plastic baggie, whereas it takes double, *as in four seconds*, to rinse out the reusable kind. Who has that kind of time?! Not to mention how long it takes to walk back to the car when we realize that

---

[26] Remarks, meeting with political, business and community leaders, Quito, Ecuador, July 7, 2015

we've left the reusable grocery bags in the trunk. And don't get me started on how long it takes to rinse out jars for the recycling bin.

4. Perhaps the biggest deterrent to living "lightly" on the earth is the sense that the little bit that we can do doesn't make that big a difference, so we wonder why we should bother doing anything at all. As author Michelle Walker wisely said, "If you think you're too small to make a difference, you've obviously never been in bed with a mosquito." What small step could you take today to live more simply in terms of waste?

Quiet your heart and enjoy His presence. . . . Think of all He's given you through creation.

What example did Jesus leave for us in terms of simple living? How can we better reflect Him to a world that is looking for something different, something that works, something that gives hope?

> *To be a follower of Christ means we should follow Him. No one lived a simpler, more unencumbered life than He. His birth was in Spartan conditions, and His life was free from the ties of possessions or money. He was born with nothing, lived with little, and died with nothing. His simplicity was not accidental. Jesus could have chosen any standard, yet He chose to live simply. . . . "Does the Bible [imply] that we are to live like a king or like the King?" asks Rev. Tom Allen. "The simplicity, sacrifice and servanthood of Jesus Christ should be our way of life, too."[27]*

Spend some time quietly before the Lord. Ask Him to reveal to you the ways in which you can authentically follow His example in terms of waste. Ask Him to help you to show your appreciation for all He's beautifully created by taking better care of it.

"Yet all is not lost. Human beings, while capable of the worst, are also capable of rising above themselves, choosing again what is good, and making a new start." -Pope Francis

---

[27] Swenson, 203.

Day Five
LESS NOISE

We live in a time when there is more noise than ever before. The Internet, cell phones, and social media have taken things to a whole new level. Kevin DeYoung explores "the power of the screen" with the following words:

> Sometimes I wonder if I'm so busy because I've come to believe the lie that busyness is the point. And nothing allows us to be busy—all the time, with anyone anywhere—like having the whole world in a little black rectangle in your pocket. In *Hamlet's Blackberry*, William Powers likens our digital age to a gigantic room. In the room are more than a billion people. But despite its size, everyone is in close proximity to everyone else. At any moment someone may come up and tap you on the shoulder—a text, a hit, a comment, a tweet, a post, a message, a new thread. Some people come up to talk business, others to complain, others to tell secrets, others to flirt, others to sell you things, others to give you information, others just to tell you what they're thinking or doing. This goes on day and night. Powers calls it a "non-stop festival of human interaction" (xii).

> We enjoy the room immensely—for awhile. But eventually we grow tired of the constant noise. We struggle to find a personal zone. Someone taps us while we're eating, while we're sleeping, while we're on a date. We even get tapped in the bathroom for crying out loud. So we decide to take a digital vacation, just a short one. But no one else seems to know where the exit is. No one else seems interested in leaving. In fact, they all seem put off that you might not want to stay. And even when you find the exit and see the enchanting world through the opening, you aren't sure what life will be like on the other side. It's a leap of faith to jump out and see what happens.[28]

How can we possibly hear God with the noise and interruptions in the room?

It might feel like we are up against something insurmountable. We might think that it's never been so hard to live the way God wants us to. I'm not so sure. I think that if the Old Testament prophet Elijah were here, he might say he had it worse. He lived at a time when Israel was ruled by King Ahab and Queen Jezebel, who led the country into a moral pit worse than had ever been seen. We read in 1 Kings 16:33, "Ahab did

---

[28] Kevin DeYoung, "Don't Let the Screen Strangle Your Soul," January 30, 2013, Gospel Coalition, http://thegospelcoalition.org/blogs/kevindeyoung/2013/01/30/dont-let-the-screen-strangle-your-soul-2-of-2/.

more to provoke the LORD, the God of Israel, to anger than any of the kings of Israel before him."

Elijah's was the sole voice that rose up and called the nation of Israel back to God. That lonely work was hard and discouraging, and got to the point where Queen Jezebel hatched a plan to have Elijah killed. This terrified Elijah, and he ran for his life. Exhausted and sick of it all, he begged God to just let him die. He'd had it. It was all just too hard.

Read 1 Kings 19:4–12.

1. What were the first two things that God provided Elijah as He began to restore him? Where did He provide these things? See 1 Kings 19:4–8.

Because we are so accustomed to the noise and exhausting pace that marks our culture, sometimes we need to begin by getting away from it all geographically for a time of rest and refreshment. This was Jesus' advice to the exhausted disciples when He said, "Come away by yourselves to a lonely place, and rest a while." (Mark 6:31) Taking the time for a silent retreat can be the greatest gift you can give yourself.

2. What did the angel say would happen if Elijah didn't get up and eat? See 1 Kings 19:7.

We also need to get up early enough to spiritually eat something, or the journey of even a day will probably be too much for us. When we rise early, we can be refreshed by the quiet, even within busy households.

3. How did God's voice come? Describe it. See 1 Kings 19:12.

God's voice wasn't in the strong, violent wind. It wasn't in the earthquake. It wasn't in the fire. All those things were loud and attention grabbing. God's voice was a gentle whisper.

Do the voices around you sometimes feel as loud as a violent wind? Unless we become quiet, unless we turn down the noise, we're going to have a hard time hearing God's still, small voice. That voice is calling us to a place of simplicity and freedom.

4. What can you do to turn down the noise in your life? As much as we'd like God to wave a magic wand and miraculously give us this "quiet" as a gift, it's far more likely that it's going to come as a result of choices that we make.

Quiet your heart and enjoy His presence. . . . Turn down the noise and listen.

"By waiting and by calm you shall be saved, in quiet and in trust shall be your strength." (Isaiah 30:15)

Isn't this the opposite of what we usually hear? We're told that we get ahead through our own hard work and tenacity. As life speeds up and gets noisy, we are terrified of the consequences of slowing and quieting down. But God promises us that it's exactly in the quiet that we'll be strengthened and saved.

Take a few moments to sit quietly before God. This could be in an adoration chapel (the quiet is truly restorative) or in your own home. Turn off the phone, the music, the television. Still your voice and listen instead. Focus on your breathing. Slow down. Just be available to God.

Conclusion

"Just that maybe . . . maybe you don't want to change the story, because you don't know what a different ending holds." —Ann Voskamp

What would it take for you to fully embrace simplicity? What kinds of changes would need to be made? Unquestionably, these sorts of changes require courage. It seems so much safer to just keep going, doing the same thing day after day. Maybe we lack the courage to make radical changes because we can't picture how amazing life would feel if it all became simpler.

What are we missing out on in the complexity of our lives? With all the hurry, multitasking, and anxiety, are we settling for superficial relationships, meaningless activity, and lack of peace? In the words of musician Audrey Assad, "Love moves slow." But we rush past, and the opportunities to love are lost.
It all begins with small choices: the decision to say no to things that might be good but will complicate our lives to a degree that we'll lose inner peace; the decision to live with margin in our use of time, our emotions, our finances, our relationships; the decision to stop pursuing the life that the world promises will bring us satisfaction, and instead pursue the things that God says matter most.

God will give us the grace for that first small step. As we obey, the grace will continue to be poured into us, and we'll discover that God is providing us the strength we need to swim upstream to a better life, a different ending.

My Resolution

In what specific way will I apply what I learned in this lesson?

Examples:

1. Every day this week, I'll find ten things in my house that I will give away.

2. Instead of treating the earth as if it'll be here forever, regardless of what we do to it, I'll pick one concrete action (that I will pray will become a habit) to live more lightly on the earth.

3. I'll turn down the noise in my life in one practical way for the week. This may be turning off my cell phone at six o'clock each night until the morning, not listening

to the radio in the car, or rising before my family so I have uninterrupted time with God.

My Resolution:

Catechism Clips

CCC 373 In God's plan man and woman have the vocation of "subduing" the earth as stewards of God. This sovereignty is not to be an arbitrary and destructive domination. God calls man and woman, made in the image of the Creator "who loves everything that exists," to share in his providence toward other creatures; hence their responsibility for the world God has entrusted to them.

CCC 1723 The beatitude we are promised confronts us with decisive moral choices. It invites us to purify our hearts of bad instincts and to seek the love of God above all else. It teaches us that true happiness is not found in riches or well-being, in human fame or power, or in any human achievement—however beneficial it may be—such as science, technology, and art, or indeed in any creature, but in God alone, the source of every good and of all love:

> All bow down before wealth. Wealth is that to which the multitude of men pay an instinctive homage. They measure happiness by wealth; and by wealth they measure respectability. . . . It is a homage resulting from a profound faith . . . that with wealth he may do all things. Wealth is one idol of the day and notoriety is a second. . . . Notoriety, or the making of a noise in the world—it may be called "newspaper fame"—has come to be considered a great good in itself, and a ground of veneration.

Verse Study

See Appendix 2 for instructions on how to complete a verse study.

Exodus 14:14

1. Verse:

2. Paraphrase:

3. Questions:

4. Cross-references:

5. Personal Application:

 NOTES

Lesson 5

BALANCE THROUGH SURRENDER

Introduction

Some people are just born with an iron will. Take my second-born, for example. Laeka could have been the poster child for the "strong-willed child." I can mention him by name because he is now so completely delightful that we just laugh at the horror stories of his early years. So don't feel sorry for him when I dish the dirt; he gives permission.

It started when he refused to be weaned, became more evident when he refused to eat anything that wasn't white from ages one to two, and just continued to build steam as our wills collided during potty training. My mother advised me to stay steady at the wheel, *never letting him win*. She promised that if I paid my dues in the early years, I'd later enjoy him as a teenager, but if I gave in when he was little, that iron will would reemerge during the teenage years and be a terrifying force to be reckoned with. So I did the best I could. But I was *tired*.

During a particularly challenging season with Laeka (who am I kidding—that season lasted pretty much up until age five) we had someone staying with us for a month while her house was being built. She didn't have children yet, and I somehow doubt that the following would have happened if she had already been tasting the fruits of mommyhood. Anyway, Laeka was spending lunchtime as he usually did, refusing to eat the food on his plate. Our houseguest looked over at him and said, "Laeka, you can't leave the table until you eat all the food on your plate." Being a pathetic people-pleaser who hates conflict, I didn't say anything. I didn't want to embarrass her, and I didn't want her to think that I let Laeka get away with wasting food, so I unwisely backed her up.

"That's right, Laeka. You need to eat it all." Now, this was a rather unrealistic expectation. And I knew it. At this point in his young life, Laeka was no sooner going to eat all the food on his plate than he was going to switch from one brand of peach juice to another (don't ask—long story).

The battle lines were drawn. Laeka's strong will was experiencing its finest hour. Or should I say *hours*? He sat at that table for about four hours, sitting, then lying arched over the chair, then slumped over the table. It didn't matter how much I enticed him with wonderful things he could do if he would just eat his food. I finally gave up and threw the lunch away.

Some of us have a will as strong as Laeka's, and some of us are more compliant—but we *all* struggle to surrender what we want in exchange for what God wants. We want what we want, when we want it, how we want it. Moving from being self-centered to being God-centered does not come naturally.

Imagine playing tug-of-war with God. We know that we wouldn't be reflecting a balanced life if we constantly experienced a yanking back and forth—my way, then God's way, my way, then God's. But we're wrong if we think balance occurs when there's tension, the result of both sides pulling equally. The balanced life comes when we are drawn over to God's side. He pulls us toward His will, not because He wants to win, but because He wants us to "win the life that is true life." (1 Timothy 6:19) We don't need to be afraid to surrender. There is a life of abundance awaiting those who give control over to God, and it's described in 1 Corinthians 2:9 as "What eye has not seen, and ear has not heard, and what has not entered the human heart." In other words, we can't even imagine what God has prepared for us. It's just that good.

What is God asking of you today? You can stay at the table, determined to get your own way. Or you can say yes to God, making an act of courage and trust. It's only then that you will experience the abundant life that isn't only balanced, but is the pathway to happiness.

Day One
WHOM ARE WE SURRENDERING TO?

1. No one willingly surrenders to someone who doesn't have his or her best interests at heart. When we lack trust in someone, we want to protect ourselves or control the situation rather than surrender. On what basis is God worthy of our trust? What do we learn from the following verses about the One who asks us to surrender to Him?

   "Good and upright is the LORD." (Psalm 25:8)
   "Taste and see that the LORD is good; happy is the man who takes refuge in him." (Psalm 34:8, RSV)
   "Praise the LORD for the LORD is good!" (Psalm 135:3)
   "The LORD is good to all, and his compassion is over all that he has made." (Psalm 145:9, RSV)

   We can trust Him because God is _____.

   "You are precious in my eyes and honored, and I love you." (Isaiah 43:4)

   "For God so loved the world that He gave His only Son, so that everyone who believes in him might not perish but might have eternal life. For God did not send his Son into the world to condemn the world, but that the world might be saved through Him." (John 3:16, 17)

   We can trust Him because God _____ us.

2. Which words of Jesus in the Garden of Gethsemane summarize what it means to surrender? See Mark 14:32–36.

3. It isn't easy to surrender. It's hard to let go of what we want and instead embrace what God has given. Jesus walked the path before us, and gave us an example to follow. Describe what it meant for Him to yield to God's will. Does knowing what Jesus surrendered for your sake make it easier to surrender to Him?

Because God is good, He will never ask us to surrender anything unless it is for our benefit. His motives are always pure. His love for us combined with His ability to know all things means that He can look ahead and know exactly what will be best for us today and tomorrow. When we struggle with doubt, wondering if God is trustworthy, we need to look at the cross. That's where He proved the extent of His love. He holds nothing back that is for our good.

The enemy of our soul does all he can to convince us otherwise. He does his best to make us think that God is out to steal all our joy and fun. C. S. Lewis highlights this in his book *The Screwtape Letters*. In the book, Screwtape (the devil) trains his nephew in the best ways to keep Christians from experiencing the wonderful lives God has planned for them. Screwtape describes surrender in the following way: "When He [God] talks of their losing their selves, He means only abandoning the clamour of self-will; once they have done that, He really gives them back all their personality, and boasts (I am afraid, sincerely) that when they are wholly His they will be more themselves than ever."[29]

4. Do you ever worry that if you surrender your life to God, your life or personality will somehow be diminished? In what way? Did anything in today's lesson make you look at things differently?

---

[29] C. S. Lewis, *The Screwtape Letters* (Old Tappan, NJ: Fleming H. Revell, 1979), 59.

Quiet your heart and enjoy His presence. . . . Rest on the foundation of His unchanging love and goodness.

"When we say 'God' we confess a constant, unchangeable being, always the same, faithful and just, without any evil. It follows that we must necessarily accept his words and have complete faith in him and acknowledge his authority. He is almighty, merciful, and infinitely beneficent. Who could not place all hope in him? Who could not love him when contemplating the treasures of goodness and love he has poured out on us?" (CCC 2086)

Only a fool would surrender to someone he or she knew nothing about. God doesn't ask us to surrender to some unknown force or being. He asks us to surrender to Him—*our loving Father whose greatest desire is to see us safe, fulfilled, and experiencing supernatural peace. When we are struggling to surrender to God, we need to shift our focus away from what we are clinging to and trying to keep, and instead focus on God. The more we know Him, the easier it will be to trust Him and release our lives into His capable hands. He is unchanging—" always the same, faithful and just, without any evil." This is one of the reasons it's so important to study the Bible, because He reveals His character through His Word. Take some time to meditate on the attributes of God that make Him worthy of your trust. Thank Him for His unchanging goodness toward you.*

Day Two
WHY DO WE SURRENDER?

When we surrender all we have to Christ, we are simply giving Him what He deserves. He gave us His life; we respond by giving Him ours. In addition, when we surrender, we are on the surest path to both holiness and happiness.

1. Now that Christ has freed us from our bondage to sin, what have we become in relation to God? See Romans 6:22.

Most people reading Romans 6:22 will have an adverse reaction. Who wants to be called a slave? We'd rather hear about being God's beloved daughters. Make no mistake, we *are* God's beloved daughters and have "received a spirit of adoption through which we cry 'Abba, Father!' The Spirit itself bears witness with our spirit that we are children of God." (Romans 8:15–16) But Scripture also says that we are God's slaves. Both *slave* and *daughter* describe our true identity.

Recognizing ourselves as slaves or servants of God may not feel warm and fuzzy, but we need to accept this truth. If we don't acknowledge God's greatness and superiority to us, we'll justify all sorts of compromise. When God asks something of us that is hard or seems unnecessary, we'll assume that we have the right to react any way we feel like. In the words of Kyle Idleman:

> My concern is that many of our churches in America have gone from being sanctuaries to becoming stadiums. And every week all the fans come to the stadium where they cheer for Jesus but have no interest in truly following him. The biggest threat to the church today is fans who call themselves Christians but aren't actually interested in following Christ. They want to be close enough to Jesus to get all the benefits, but not so close that it requires anything from them.[30]

God is neither a celebrity we admire nor the captain of a successful sports team. He is *Lord*, which literally translated means He is the master. He doesn't need fans; He wants followers. As the King of the Universe, He requires that we follow Him by releasing to Him all that we are and all we possess.

2. How did Jesus describe the process of surrender in John 12:24–26? What did He say would result from surrender (dying to self)?

> Whoever makes a habit of prayer should think only of doing everything to conform his will to God's. Be assured that in this conformity consists the highest perfection we can attain, and those who practice it with the greatest care will be favored by God's greatest gift and will make the quickest progress in the interior life. Do not imagine there are other secrets. All our good consists in this." —Saint Teresa of Avila

---

[30] Kyle Idleman, *Not a Fan: Becoming a Completely Committed Follower of Jesus* (Grand Rapids, MI: Zondervan, 2011), 25.

3. If we aren't willing to surrender our desires and needs to God, we'll become convinced that the only way we can be happy is to have those desires and needs satisfied. This places us on very shaky ground. Our circumstances will always be subject to change, and as a result, our happiness will rise and fall. But when we submit our will to God's, when we want what He wants, we can receive anything from His hand as a gift. How does Saint Paul tell us to respond to all circumstances? What part does surrendering to God's will play in these instructions? See 1 Thessalonians 5:16–18.

4. What are some common excuses we use in order to avoid surrendering to God?

Quiet your heart and enjoy His presence. . . . You belong to the One who loves you like no other.

One of the most common excuses we use to avoid surrendering to God doesn't sound like an excuse at all. We might express enthusiasm over the idea of surrender, or we might acknowledge how right it is that God would ask this or that of us, but we determine to do it later. We haven't outright refused, so we figure God appreciates our good intentions. We're sure we'll do it tomorrow.

If we really want to grow in the spiritual life, we'll determine to obey God immediately when He calls. We'll recognize that He has every right to ask anything of us. "For you are not your own . . . you have been purchased at a price." (1 Corinthians 6:19–20) We weren't purchased "with perishable things like silver or gold but with the precious blood of Christ." (1 Peter 1:18)

Ask God if there is something He wants from you. Sit in quiet to allow Him the chance to impress some thoughts on your heart. When you know that God is asking you to surrender and obey, do it straightaway. Don't put off something until tomorrow that could be done today.

Day Three
WHAT ARE WE SURRENDING?

1. Surrendering is perhaps the highest form of worship. We aren't just to worship with our words. What does Saint Paul challenge us to surrender in Romans 12:1? What are some practical ways we can live out that challenge?

2. We aren't just to surrender our bodies. What else does Saint Paul teach us to offer to God? See Romans 12:2. What are some practical ways we can live this out?

3. What does God want us to surrender most of all? See Proverbs 23:26.

What is the heart? The heart is the place where we keep our dreams, our love, our agendas. It's the driving force behind what we do. It's where our motives are rooted. God wants our hearts more than anything. When we offer our hearts, we open ourselves up to His transforming power. We are changed in the core of our being so that we begin to want what God wants, when He wants it, how He wants it. In the words of K. P. Yohannan, "You see, by choosing to come into His presence, we leave aside our agenda and prepare ourselves to submit to His yoke. In His presence we are changed; the independent spirit is substituted for His will and His ways. Our hearts change as a deep transformation takes place within."[31]

---

[31] K. P. Yohannan, *The Lord's Work Done in the Lord's Way* (Carrollton, TX: GFA Books, 2004), 38.

4. The story is told of an unusual baptismal practice involving the Knights Templar. When the knights were baptized, they carried their swords with them. Their bodies would be immersed, but they held their swords above the water. In doing so, they offered God much of who they were, but held back the sword. That part of their lives would remain under their control.[32] What are you tempted to hold out of the water? What is the hardest thing for you to surrender to Christ?

Quiet your heart and enjoy His presence. . . . Offer Him your all.

We read in the Old Testament of Job, a man who suffered like no other. After losing his possessions and all his children, he was able to say, "Naked I came forth from my mother's womb, and naked shall I go back there. The LORD gave and the LORD has taken away; blessed be the name of the LORD!" (Job 1:21) Could we say the same? If God allowed us to lose the one thing that we'd hold out of the water, could we still say, "Blessed be the name of the Lord"? Do we love Him for who He is or for what He gives us? Take some time to meditate on this question. Ask God to help you have a heart like the Blessed Mother's when she said, "Behold, I am the servant of the Lord; let it be to me according to your word." (Luke 1:38)

Day Four
HOW DO WE SURRENDER A SITUATION WE'RE DESPERATE TO CHANGE?

The Christian life is full of paradoxes. The least shall be greatest.[33] A life of self-denial is the fullest life.[34] We are strongest when we're weakest.[35] Today we'll look at the paradox of surrender: We experience freedom when we embrace our limitations. Father Jacques Philippe wrote the following about this seeming contradiction in his book *Interior Freedom*:

---

[32] Idleman, 202.
[33] Matthew 23:11–12
[34] Matthew 10:39
[35] 2 Corinthians 12:10

To achieve true interior freedom we must train ourselves to accept, peacefully and willingly, plenty of things that seem to contradict our freedom. This means consenting to our personal limitations, our weaknesses, our powerlessness, this or that situation that life imposes on us, and so on. We find it difficult to do this, because we feel a natural revulsion for situations we cannot control. But the fact is that the situations that really make us grow are precisely those we do not control.[36]

He goes on to describe the various ways that we can respond to these situations that we find undesirable. We can **rebel** against them, refusing to accept our current circumstances. We might move on from rebellion to a place of **resignation**. While this is progress, it still falls short of how God wants us to respond. "Resignation doesn't include hope. Resignation is a declaration of powerlessness that goes no further."[37] Father Philippe challenges us to move on to a place of **consent**. This is an attitude of the heart that accepts the situation and looks for the good hidden in it. *The key to consent is the virtue of hope.* When we are struggling to surrender a circumstance that we desperately wish would change, hope is the virtue we need to focus on and develop.

1. How is hope described in Romans 8:24–25 and Hebrews 6:18–19?

2. When we are in the midst of a circumstance that we wish would change, what should we be hoping for? See Romans 8:28.

3. How is hope expressed and nourished? See CCC 1820.

---

[36] Jacques Philippe, *Interior Freedom* (New York: Scepter Publishers, 2007), 28–29.
[37] Ibid., 30.

4. Hope, by definition, requires a focus on the future. How far into the future should our focus be? See CCC 1821.

Quiet your heart and enjoy His presence. . . . Hope will not disappoint.

When our hearts are filled with hope, we can look past our current circumstances to the good that will come in the future. Embracing hope is a choice. The opposite of the virtue of hope is worry or anger over current circumstances. While those are natural reactions to situations that we hate, they lead us down a path toward darkness and discouragement.

In her devotional, Streams in the Desert, L.B. Cowman contrasts the difference between a spirited horse bucking against its yoke and only hurting itself in the process, and a canary in a cage that sits on its perch and sings the most beautiful song imaginable, despite its captivity. What results from our unfavorable circumstances depends on our perspective. She writes:

> *No calamity will ever bring only evil to us, if we will immediately take it in fervent prayer to God. Even as we take shelter beneath a tree during a downpour of rain, we may unexpectedly find fruit on its branches. And when we flee to God, taking refuge beneath the shadow of His wing, we will always find more in Him than we have ever before seen or known.*[38]

Hope allows us to look beyond what is right in front of us to see potential, to continue dreaming, and to patiently wait for God to act. It isn't a passive wishfulness, it's an active forward focus that believes in God's promises. We can rest with a spirit of expectation because "he who made the promise is trustworthy" (Hebrews 10:23).

---

[38] L. B. Cowman, *Streams in the Desert*, ed. James Reimann (Grand Rapids, MI: Zondervan, 1997), 415–16.

Day Five
HOW DO WE SURRENDER WHAT WE DEEPLY LOVE?

1. Meditating on the surrender of the Blessed Mother, read the Scriptures below and note what she surrendered to God at these particular points of her life.

   Luke 1:25–28

   Luke 2:6–7

   Luke 2:41–49

2. What was the most difficult time of surrender for the Blessed Mother? See John 19:25.

Does it still count as surrender if you can't do anything to change the situation? Most definitely. Although Mary couldn't rescue her son, she could have rebelled in her heart against the reality of this unimaginably horrific situation. She could have screamed out to Jesus to call on the angels to rescue Him. But this isn't how she responded. She stayed. She didn't leave His side. She offered Him strength and comfort through her surrender to God's will. She allowed Him the freedom to obey God without having to worry about what His obedience would cost her. There was nothing she loved more than her Son, and she offered Him back to the One who gave Him to her in the first place.

3. In order to surrender to God what we love most, we have to trust that He will take care of who or what we offer. In order to trust Him, we need to acknowledge the truth of God's words in Isaiah 55:8–9: "For my thoughts are not your thoughts, nor are your ways my ways. . . . For as the heavens are higher than the

earth, so are my ways higher than your ways, my thoughts higher than your thoughts." Is there an area of your life where you struggle to remember this?

4. We hesitate to surrender what we love to God because we are afraid. We fear that He will allow something other than what we would choose. Think of something that's hard to surrender to God. Then read Jesus' words to Peter, receiving them as His words for you: "What I am doing, you do not understand now, but you will understand later."[39] Can you exercise hope today even though you can't see the why behind God's actions?

Quiet your heart and enjoy His presence. . . . He is worthy of your trust.

"There is no fear in love, but perfect love drives out fear." (1 John 4:18)

In order to place what is most precious to us in God's capable hands, we have to keep our focus on His sacrificial, never-diminishing love. When we rest under His tender, pure, compassionate, and true love, we feel secure. That security reminds us that we don't need to be afraid. God is in control. He loves us. He has the big picture. We do not.

Saint John was given a powerful vision of Jesus in the book of Revelation. He described it as follows:

> *Then I saw the heavens opened, and there was a white horse; its rider was called "Faithful and True." He judges and wages war in righteousness. His eyes were like a fiery flame, and on his head were many diadems. He had a name inscribed that no one knows except himself. He wore a cloak that had been dipped in blood, and his name was called the Word of God. The armies of heaven followed him, mounted on white horses and wearing clean white linen. . . . He has a name written on his cloak and on his thigh, "King of kings and Lord of lords." (Revelation 19:11–16)*

---

[39] John 13:7

The King of kings and Lord of lords is "Faithful and True." He will never leave or forsake us. Our lives and all we hold most dear are safe with Him. Take some time to picture Jesus on His majestic white horse. He comes to rescue you. He wants to rescue those you love most, as well. They are each on their own journey, and the way He will capture their hearts is between Him and them. Release your loved one to His care. There's no safer place than in His hands.

Conclusion

"One does not surrender a life in an instant. That which is lifelong can only be surrendered in a lifetime." —Elisabeth Elliot

Surrendering is a lifelong process. We do it with little decisions and big ones. We step forward in faith, and sometimes step back in fear. Through it all, Jesus stays by our side, joyful beyond measure when our surrender reveals our trust in Him. It's the best thank-you we can give Him for all He's done for us, and He receives it as such.

We're also surrounded by a "great cloud of witnesses"[40]—the saints who cheer us on from heaven. They've walked the road of surrender before us and promise us that it's worth every obedient step. One of those saints is Thérèse of Lisieux. Her words in Story of a Soul can both comfort us in our weakness and challenge us to progress in the process of yielding our will to God. She describes the following interaction with her sisters in a way that reminds us that we're all works in progress. If she could change, so can we!

> One day Leonie, no doubt thinking she was too old to play with dolls, came to us both with a basket filled with their clothes, ribbons, and other odds and ends. Her own doll was on top. She said: "Here you are darlings. Take what you want." Celine took a little bundle of silk braid. I thought for a moment, then stretched out my hand and declared "I choose everything," and without more ado, I carried off the lot. Everyone thought this quite fair.

> This episode sums up the whole of my life. Much later, when I understood what perfection was, I realized that to become a saint one must suffer a great deal, always seek what is best, and forget oneself. I understood that there were many kinds of sanctity and that each soul was free to respond to the approaches of Our Lord and to do little or much for Him—in other words, to make a choice among the sacrifices He demands. Then, just as when I was a

---

[40] Hebrews 12:1

child, I cried: "My God, I choose all. I do not want to be a saint by halves. I am not afraid to suffer for You. I fear only one thing—that I should keep my own will. So take it, for I choose all that you will."[41]

This is the secret of the saints. This is what Saint Paul was talking about when he said, "It is no longer I who live, but Christ who lives in me." (Galatians 2:20) This is "less of me, and more of God." It's the path to holiness, and the source of true happiness. It's the abundant life God is just waiting for you to live!

My Resolution

In what specific way will I apply what I learned in this lesson?

Examples:

1. Even if I feel my life circumstances are confining, I will look for a specific way I can "sing like a canary" right where I am.

2. When I'm finding it hard to surrender, I will thank God for ten things that He has done that remind me how trustworthy He is.

3. I'll take time each day to pray this prayer of surrender: "Take, Lord, and receive, all my liberty, my memory, my understanding, and my entire will, all that I have and possess. You have given all to me. To You, O Lord, I return it. All is Yours. Dispose of it wholly according to Your will. Give me Your love and Your grace, for this is sufficient for me." (Prayer of Saint Ignatius)

My Resolution:

---

[41] St. Thérèse of Lisieux, *Story of a Soul: The Autobiography of St. Thérèse of Lisieux*, trans. John Clarke (New York: Doubleday, 2001), 9.

Catechism Clips

CCC 1820 Christian hope unfolds from the beginning of Jesus' preaching in the proclamation of the *beatitudes*. The beatitudes raise our hope toward heaven as the new Promised Land; they trace the path that leads through the trials that await the disciples of Jesus. But through the merits of Jesus Christ and of his Passion, God keeps us in the "hope that does not disappoint." Hope is the "sure and steadfast anchor of the soul . . . that enters . . . where Jesus has gone as a forerunner on our behalf." Hope is also a weapon that protects us in the struggle of salvation: "Let us . . . put on the breastplate of faith and charity, and for a helmet the hope of salvation." It affords us joy even under trial: "Rejoice in your hope, be patient in tribulation." Hope is expressed and nourished in prayer, especially in the Our Father, the summary of everything that hope leads us to desire.

CCC 1821 We can therefore hope in the glory of heaven promised by God to those who love him and do his will. In every circumstance, each one of us should hope, with the grace of God, to persevere "to the end" and to obtain the joy of heaven, as God's eternal reward for the good works accomplished with the grace of Christ. In hope, the Church prays for "all men to be saved." She longs to be united with Christ, her Bridegroom, in the glory of heaven:

> Hope, O my soul, hope. You know neither the day nor the hour. Watch carefully, for everything passes quickly, even though your impatience makes doubtful what is certain, and turns a very short time into a long one. Dream that the more you struggle, the more you prove the love that you bear your God, and the more you will rejoice one day with your Beloved, in a happiness and rapture that can never end.

Verse Study

See Appendix 2 for instructions on how to complete a verse study.

Matthew 19:29

1. Verse:

2. Paraphrase:

3. Questions:

4. Cross-references:

5. Personal Application:

NOTES

Lesson 6

BALANCE IN OUR THOUGHT LIFE

Introduction

Can you imagine how mortifying it would be if all our thoughts were broadcast live and anyone could hear them? Think of all the things that race through our minds—negative thoughts about ourselves, wishing our circumstances were different, worries about the future, fearful thoughts, angry thoughts, critical thoughts about other people, the rehashing of past hurts. Sure, we have plenty of good thoughts, and we wouldn't care if people knew some of those, but what if they could hear all of the negative ones, too? Thankfully, our thoughts are contained within us. They are private. They are ours, and no one can access them without our consent.

But does that mean that what we do with them doesn't matter? As long as thoughts just stay in our heads, are they harmless? Does it matter what we think?

Jesus answers these questions with the following words: "Love the Lord your God with all your heart, with all your soul, and with all your mind." (Matthew 22:37) If the thoughts in our minds aren't the ones God wants us to dwell on, we're going to have a hard time loving Him and the people He places in our paths. Our thoughts directly impact our actions. They matter a great deal to God.

Jerusha Clark, author of *Every Thought Captive*, writes:

> We sin, in large part, because we hold on to and live out of toxic beliefs. So whether we are aware of the depths and brokenness of our thoughts or not, they are very real, and they influence us more than we ever know. Many of our thoughts, unfortunately, are both negative and untrue. At different points in their lives, most women have believed poisonous lies such as these: I'm not good enough. What others think about me defines who I am. I am the sum of my accomplishments and my relationships. We have believed a multitude of

other self-defeating falsities as well, lies that have hijacked and poisoned our minds.[42]

Even when we recognize that our thoughts matter, we might feel that we just can't help thinking certain things. We may feel powerless to get a grip on the fears that prey on our minds. Perhaps we don't know how to keep our emotions from ruling our thoughts. Many of us feel a constant barrage of negative thoughts about ourselves, and we just don't know what to do about it.

The good news is we are not victims of our thought patterns. We have a choice, and with God's help, we can come to a place where we learn to control what we hold in our minds. We do not need to be slaves to our emotions, our past, or our worries. Our minds can be transformed.

Day One
THE BATTLE IS IN THE MIND

There is a battle that rages every day in our minds. God appeals to us to think the thoughts that will lead to good actions and attitudes. We also have an enemy who pulls us in the opposite direction. In the event that we think of evil as an abstract concept, the *Catechism of the Catholic Church* tells us, "Evil is not an abstraction, but refers to a person, Satan, the Evil One, the angel who opposes God. The devil is the one who 'throws himself across' God's plan and his work of salvation accomplished in Christ." (CCC 2851)

1. Philippians 4:8 contains specific instructions regarding our thought life. What eight types of thoughts does God want us to dwell on?

2. Which types of thoughts aren't consistent with Philippians 4:8?

---

[42] Jerusha Clark, *Every Thought Captive* (Colorado Springs: Th1nk, 2006), 14–15.

3. Read John 8:44. How is Satan described? What insight does this give you into the types of thoughts he will tempt you to dwell on?

So how do we determine whether a thought is the truth or a lie? The more you attune your ear and heart to God's voice, the easier it will be to identify truth. Your ability to recognize God's voice will grow in direct proportion to your knowledge of Scripture and your sensitivity to the prompting of the Holy Spirit. We grow in sensitivity to the prompting of the Holy Spirit through confession (breaking down the barrier of sin), through prayer (asking God to give us greater sensitivity to the Holy Spirit), and then through obedience (acting immediately on what God has shown us to do).

We also need to learn to inwardly quiet down. There's a lot of "chatter" that goes on in our heads that's not truth. It's just a mixture of our memories, our desires, our motivations, and our perceptions of reality. We have got to discipline ourselves to sit in quiet, asking God to speak to us. When a thought pops into our heads (like what we need to buy from the grocery store), we can quickly write it down, then bring our focus back to God. Ask Him to give you "the mind of Christ" (1 Corinthians 2:16) and to help you bring your thoughts in line with His.

4. What negative thought do you struggle with most often? Take that thought to its furthest point. For example, you may often find yourself thinking, "I'm overwhelmed and I'm never going to get everything done." Take that thought to the next point by asking, "So what will happen if I never get everything done?" You might reply, "I'll fail. I'll let people down." Take it to the next point by asking, "So what happens if I fail?" You might reply, "I'll feel like a loser. Like I can't get my act together. Like I'm worthless." That final thought is the toxic one. That's the thought that needs to be battled and compared to the truth. *Is it true* that if I fail I am worthless? Is that thought consistent with what I read in Scripture? It's at the furthest point of the thought that we begin to find the deeper issue, the issue that needs to be held up to the truth of God's Word. Take your negative thought to its furthest point. Identify the toxic thought at its root. Compare that thought to the truth you know from Scripture.

Ask God to bring healing to that place of negativity.

My negative thought:

Take it to the next point:

Take it to the furthest point:

What is the toxic thought at the root? Is that thought true? Is it consistent with Scripture?

Quiet your heart and enjoy His presence. . . . Listen to Him affirming His love for you.

Every day, you need to begin by saturating your mind with truth. Countless negative messages will make their way into your mind each day. It's your responsibility to make sure that you begin the day with a mind loaded with what is true, honorable, just, pure, lovely, gracious, excellent, and praiseworthy. Imagine yourself being showered by God's love. Throughout your day, rest under His tender gaze.

The truth is: HE LOVES YOU WITH AN EVERLASTING LOVE.

The truth is: THERE IS NOTHING YOU CAN DO TO INCREASE OR DECREASE THAT LOVE.

The truth is: YOU DON'T HAVE TO PROVE YOUR WORTH. JESUS ALREADY PROVED YOU ARE WORTH EVERYTHING ON THE CROSS.

Day Two
REJECT AND REPLACE

One of the ways that the enemy of our soul gets us to believe lies is by convincing us that if we *feel* something, it must be true. The truth is, we can't always trust our feelings. We read in Jeremiah 17:9 that "more torturous than anything is the human heart, beyond remedy; who can understand it?" Of course, with God, all things are possible and nothing is without remedy. But the verse does illustrate that we're going to have to put in some effort if peace is going to reign in our hearts

Instead of seeking to determine if something is true based on our feelings, we need to hold up a thought and compare it to God's truth. If the thought isn't consistent with God's truth, we need to reject it and replace it with a different one.

1. Saint Paul describes in 2 Corinthians 10:3–6 the unique battle a Christian faces. Explain that spiritual battle in your own words. Then write what we are supposed to do with every single one of our thoughts.

2. In 2 Corinthians 10:4 we read that our weapons "are not of flesh but are enormously powerful." Describe our weapons and armor. See Ephesians 6:10–17.

If we ignore any one of those pieces of armor or leave our weapons at home, we're going to have a really tough time in the battle to take every thought captive. But with truth, righteousness, the gospel, faith, salvation, and Scripture, we have all the weapons we need.

3. As you filter your thoughts (instead of just letting them roam freely in your mind), hold each one up and compare it to truth. Discard the lies or negative thoughts. But don't stop there. If you simply reject the thought but don't replace it with something else, two seconds later you'll be thinking the same negative thing. The key is to replace the negative thought with God's truth. Read each of the following negative thoughts, then record the truth-filled Bible verse that can be planted in your mind instead.

Reject: God is not really enough.
Replace: Psalm 23:1

Reject: I'm worthless.
Replace: Isaiah 43:4

Reject: What we look like matters more than who we are inside.
Replace: 1 Samuel 16:7

Reject: God can't forgive what I've done.
Replace: 1 John 1:9

Quiet your heart and enjoy His presence. . . . Sitting at His feet is empowering.

Nothing delights Satan more than a woman ruled by her untamed thoughts and emotions. But a woman who recognizes that she's got powerhouse weapons that are strong enough to tear down anything Satan seeks to throw in her path? That's the kind of woman he wishes would just stay in bed.

Do you realize the power that is within you? Do you recognize the "surpassing greatness of his power" [43] that is in us through the indwelling Holy Spirit? Do you know this is the same power that raised Jesus from the dead? "The one who is in you is greater than the one who is in the world." (1 John 4:4)

But it's as we sit at God's feet that we soak up that power. This is one of the reasons we have got to make time for prayer. Skipping prayer means we're heading out into the day with feeble weapons that are no match for what our enemy might throw at us. Take some time today to be filled with the power of the Holy Spirit. Ask Him to fill every part of you—from the top of your head to the tip of your toes. Then go out in God's strength!

Day Three
CHECK THE ENTRY POINTS

We'll save ourselves a lot of trouble if we take care to guard what gets into our minds in the first place. The Trojan horse seemed like such a great spoil of war, but with Greek warriors hidden inside, it brought about the destruction of Troy. In that same way, we can either invite all sorts of garbage into our minds or wisely avoid the things that expose us to fresh negative material.

1. What should we guard according to Matthew 6:22–23?

2. What should we guard according to 1 Corinthians 15:33 and Proverbs 22:24–25?

3. What should we guard according to Proverbs 18:8 and 20:19?

---

[43] Ephesians 1:19–20

4. Which of the entry points to your mind are often left unguarded? What you look at? Whom you spend time with? What you listen to? Where you go? What can you do to better protect yourself?

Quiet your heart and enjoy His presence. . . . This is a safe, protected place.

Even though we have enormous spiritual power within us, we still need to guard the entry points to our minds. There are some situations that are guaranteed to take us down a bad mental path. Choosing to stay home rather than putting ourselves in a place where we're probably going to be filled with wrong thoughts isn't cowardly. It's wise. Recognizing that certain friends bring out the worst in us and reducing our time with them is prudent. This doesn't mean that we should retreat into a Christian bubble; we are meant to be the sweet fragrance of Christ to people who don't know Him. But we need to pay attention to whether we are being the influencers or the influenced. Ask God to help you identify anything that needs adjusting in this area of your life.

Day Four
REFUSE TO WORRY

"Can any of you by worrying add a single moment to your life-span?" (Matthew 6:27)

1. What does God promise if we will take our worries to Him? See Philippians 4:6–7. Tucked in the middle of verse 6 is a description of the way we should bring our worries to God. What is it?

2. When we are worrying about our what-ifs, we are usually imagining the worst-case scenario apart from God's presence. Without realizing it, what we are often saying is, "I don't think you can help me through this, Lord. I think this problem would be too big for you." This is a lie that we need to reject the minute it comes into our minds. Then we need to replace the lie with the truth. What truth is found in Isaiah 43:1–2? Because of that truth, how should we think of our worst-case scenario worries?

3. What do we learn from Ecclesiastes 7:14 and CCC 2115 regarding our desire to see into the future?

4. We can't know everything the future holds, but there are certain things we can count on. Step 1: Read the following verses, and record what we *do* know about the future. Step 2: Write how that knowledge can help us with our worries.

   John 16:33

   Isaiah 41:10

   Isaiah 54:10

   Jeremiah 29:11

Quiet your heart and enjoy His presence. . . . Bring your worries to the One who holds the whole world in His hands.

Don't stress if worries keep popping back into your mind. Just deal with them as they come. Ask God to help you replace the worrying thought with trust in Him. The Catechism tells us that reading the Psalms helps us learn to trust God more. "The prayer of the Psalms is the great school of this trust." (CCC 304) Psalms 23, 46, and 121 are great trust-building psalms. It can also be helpful to go to a friend for encouragement. "Worry weighs down the heart, but a kind word gives it joy." (Proverbs 12:25)

Bring your worries to the Lord today and place them in His hands. Prayerfully read Psalm 46, thanking God for the fact that He alone is totally worthy of our trust. He is bigger and more powerful than any of our worries.

Day Five
GOING DEEP

I would be remiss if I left you with the impression that we should always live on the surface of our emotions, never diving deeper to address what's going on in our hearts. Some of the wounds that we have experienced in the past (or are experiencing in the present) are deep and painful. When thoughts of intense hurt surface, am I suggesting that we ignore them and exchange them for thoughts of rainbows and sunshine? No. There is a big difference between dwelling on negative thoughts that are not true and facing real pain that needs healing.

1. What do you think is the difference between dwelling on negative thoughts from the past and addressing painful memories in light of God's unconditional love?

2. Satan loves to play in the shadows. He loves when things stay hidden and confused. God wants to shine light into the darkness (Psalm 112:4). Sometimes the light hurts our eyes; we don't want to look back and address painful memories. But God promises He will never leave our side, and that He wants to lead us to a place of healing and freedom. When we can name the pain in our past, its power over us starts to lessen. We realize that we can decide how we are going to respond. What happened in the past is beyond our control, but how we react to

that reality today is very much in our control. What do the following verses say to you about where God is in the midst of the processing of our pain?

"A bruised reed he will not break, and a dimly burning wick he will not quench. He will faithfully bring forth justice." (Isaiah 42:3, NLT)

"The Lord is close to the brokenhearted, and saves those whose spirit is crushed." (Psalm 34:19)

"You are my fortress, my refuge in time of trouble." (Psalm 59:17)

It can be scary to journey back to our place of woundedness. We might prefer to just not think about it. But God wants us to be able to think about what was true and real without those thoughts having a hold on us. He wants us to walk in freedom. Sometimes that means we have to go back and process the past. But He never leaves us to do that alone. And when we feel too weak and afraid to go there, He reminds us, "My grace is sufficient for you, for power is made perfect in weakness." (2 Corinthians 12:9) And remember, there is nothing weak about asking for help. Taking advantage of professional help is not only wise; it's often God's chosen means to bring us to a place of healing.

3. Forgiveness is an essential step if we want to move to a place of healing. Sometimes we need to be forgiven; other times, we need to forgive. It's often said that hurting people hurt people. How does that insight, along with Luke 23:34, affect your thoughts about forgiveness?

4. What does 2 Corinthians 1:3–5 encourage us to do with the pain of our past?

Quiet your heart and enjoy His presence. . . . Bring your pain into the healing light of His love.

God never tells His suffering children to "snap out of it," "get it together," or "suck it up." He realizes that the solution isn't always just to pray more, read the Bible more, or go to church more. He comes close to us in our sorrow and pain, and offers healing. Sometimes the first step of healing feels like the washing of a cut that's filled with gravel. It hurts, and we just want to slap on a Band-Aid instead of suffering the pain of getting rid of the dirt. But if we'll trust God, He'll only do what's necessary to bring us to a place of wholeness. And remember, you're in good company. Many saints have been just where you are today. Your story isn't finished. The best is yet to come.

Conclusion

> Remember not the events of the past,
> the things of long ago consider not;
> See, I am doing something new!
> Now it springs forth, do you not perceive it?
> In the wilderness I make a way,
> In the wasteland, rivers. (Isaiah 43:18–19)

When we have gone through the process of dealing with the pain in our past, we can leave it there. We don't need to be defined by it or burdened by it. Even if the thoughts about our past are true, we can set them aside, and look forward. We worship a God who is all about fresh starts. Each day, He invites us to hit a "do over" button.

Did you struggle with worry yesterday? Start afresh today!

Did you fall back into an old pattern of sin? Fill up with God's strength today and determine to walk in victory.

Are memories of the past haunting you? Take those thoughts captive, hold them up to the truth of Scripture, and ask God to continue to heal your heart. Then fill your mind with the truth about God's unconditional love and His promise to never leave your side.

Every day, God wants to do something new in your life. Sometimes you rush around from one thing to the next, and unfortunately, often you don't perceive His actions. But He is there. He is present. No matter how much you may feel like you are lost in the wilderness, God can make a path for you to a place of freedom. Do you feel like you're in the desert, a barren wasteland? God can make rivers spring up where there is no evidence of a water source.

Even when you mess up, God can still make a way. He can take your bad choices, hurtful things people have done to you, tragedies, and loss and create a beautiful masterpiece of a life.

Choose to see God's presence in every one of your circumstances. You can trust Him with your past, present, and future.

My Resolution

In what specific way will I apply what I learned in this lesson?

Examples:

1. I will write Philippians 4:8 on an index card, carrying it around with me or putting it in strategic places (on the bathroom mirror, over the kitchen sink, on the dashboard of the car) until I have it memorized. This will allow the Holy Spirit to help me check my thoughts. Are they true? Are they real?

2. I'll read daily Psalm 23, 46, or 121 as a way to grow in trust in God.

3. If I am dealing with some deep wounds from the past or depression in the present, and I don't feel able to deal with it alone, I will make an appointment with a professional to begin the journey of healing.

My Resolution:

Catechism Clips

CCC 304 And so we see the Holy Spirit, the principal author of Sacred Scripture, often attributing actions to God without mentioning any secondary causes. This is not a "primitive mode of speech," but a profound way of recalling God's primacy and absolute Lordship over history and the world, and so of educating his people to trust in him. The prayer of the Psalms is the great school of this trust.

CCC 2115 God can reveal the future to his prophets or to other saints. Still, a sound Christian attitude consists in putting oneself confidently into the hands of Providence for whatever concerns the future, and giving up all unhealthy curiosity about it. Improvidence, however, can constitute a lack of responsibility.

CCC 2851 In this petition ["but deliver us from evil"], evil is not an abstraction, but refers to a person, Satan, the Evil One, the angel who opposes God. The devil is the one who "throws himself across" God's plan and his work of salvation accomplished in Christ.

Verse Study

See Appendix 2 for instructions on how to complete a verse study.

1 Peter 5:6-7

1. Verse:

2. Paraphrase:

3. Questions:

4. Cross-references:

5. Personal Application:

NOTES

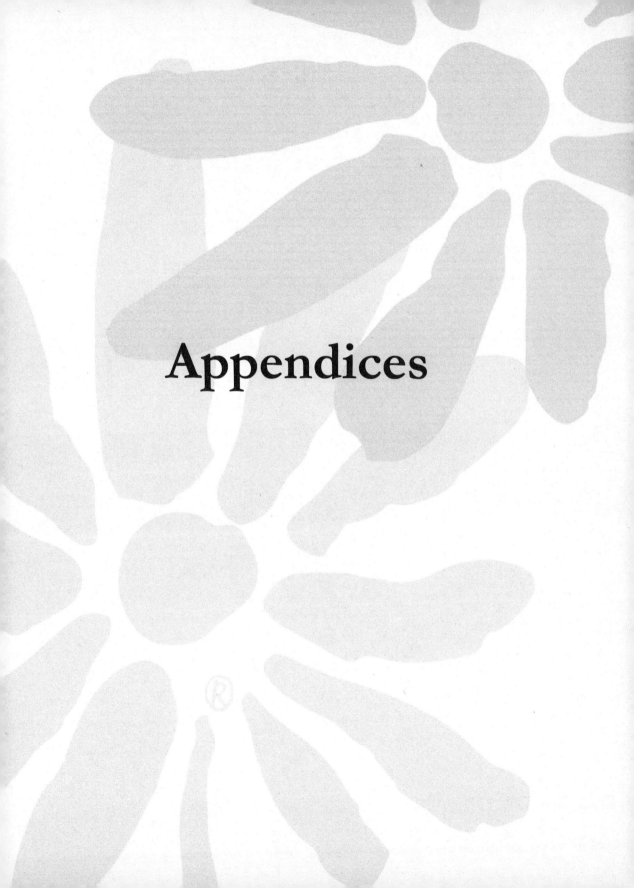

Appendices

——— NOTES ———

Appendix 1
SAINT THÉRÈSE OF LISIEUX

Patron Saint of Walking with Purpose

Saint Thérèse of Lisieux was gifted with the ability to take the riches of our Catholic faith and explain them in a way that a child could imitate. The wisdom she gleaned from Scripture ignited a love in her heart for her Lord that was personal and transforming. The simplicity of the faith that she laid out in her writings is so completely Catholic that Pope Pius XII said, "She rediscovered the Gospel itself, the very heart of the Gospel."

Walking with Purpose is intended to be a means by which women can honestly share their spiritual struggles and embark on a journey that is refreshing to the soul. It was never intended to facilitate the deepest of intellectual study of Scripture. Instead, the focus has been to help women know Christ: to know His heart, to know His tenderness, to know His mercy, and to know His love. Our logo is a little flower, and that has meaning. When a woman begins to open her heart to God, it's like the opening of a little flower. It can easily be bruised or crushed, and it must be treated with the greatest of care. Our desire is to speak to women's hearts no matter where they are in life, baggage and all, and gently introduce truths that can change their lives.

Saint Thérèse of Lisieux, the little flower, called her doctrine "the little way of spiritual childhood," and it is based on complete and unshakable confidence in God's love for us. She was not introducing new truths. She spent countless hours reading Scripture and she shared what she found, emphasizing the importance of truths that had already been divinely revealed. We can learn so much from her:

> The good God would not inspire unattainable desires; I can, then, in spite of my littleness, aspire to sanctity. For me to become greater is impossible; I must put up with myself just as I am with all my imperfections. But I wish to find the way to go to Heaven by a very straight, short, completely new little way. We are in a century of inventions: now one does not even have to take the trouble to climb the steps of a stairway; in the homes of the rich, an elevator replaces them nicely. I, too, would like to find an elevator to lift me up to Jesus, for I

am too little to climb the rough stairway of perfection. So I have looked in the books of the saints for a sign of the elevator I long for, and I have read these words proceeding from the mouth of eternal Wisdom: "He that is a little one, let him turn to me" (Proverbs 9:16). So I came, knowing that I had found what I was seeking, and wanting to know, O my God, what You would do with the little one who would answer Your call, and this is what I found:

"As one whom the mother caresses, so will I comfort you. You shall be carried at the breasts and upon the knees they shall caress you" (Isaiah 66:12–13). Never have more tender words come to make my soul rejoice. The elevator which must raise me to the heavens is Your arms, O Jesus! For that I do not need to grow; on the contrary, I must necessarily remain small, become smaller and smaller. O my God, You have surpassed what I expected, and I want to sing Your mercies. (Saint Thérèse of the Infant Jesus, *Histoire d'une Ame: Manuscrits Autobiographiques* [Paris: Éditions du Seuil, 1998], 244.)

Appendix 2
HOW TO DO A VERSE STUDY

A verse study is an exciting Bible study tool that can help to bring the Scriptures to life! By reading, reflecting on, and committing a verse to memory, we open ourselves to the Holy Spirit, who reveals very personal applications of our Lord's words and actions to our daily lives.

Learning to do a verse study is not difficult, but it can be demanding. In this Walking with Purpose™ study, a Bible verse has been selected to reinforce a theme of each lesson. To do the verse study, read the verse and then follow these simple instructions. You'll be on your way to a deeper and more personal understanding of Scripture.

- **Read the verse and the paragraph before and after the verse.**

- **Write out the selected verse.**

- **Paraphrase.**
  Write the verse using your own words. What does the verse say?

- **Ask questions.**
  Write down any questions you have about the verse. What does it say that you don't understand?

- **Use cross-references.**
  Look up other Bible verses that help to shed light on what the selected verse means. A study Bible will often list cross-references in the margin or in the study notes. Another excellent resource is Biblos.com. This website allows you to enter a specific Bible verse and it will provide many cross-references and additional insights into the passage of Scripture you selected. Record any insights you gain from the additional verses you are able to find.

- **Make a personal application.**
  What does the verse say to you personally? Is there a promise to make? a warning to heed? an example to follow? Ask God to help you find something from the verse that you can apply to your life.

The recommended Bible translations for use in Walking with Purpose™ studies are: The New American Bible, which is the translation used in the United States for the readings at Mass; The Revised Standard Version, Catholic Edition; and The Jerusalem Bible.

A SAMPLE VERSE STUDY

1. **Verse:**
   John 15:5   "I am the vine, you are the branches. Those who abide in me and I in them bear much fruit, because apart from me you can do nothing."

2. **Paraphrase:**
   Jesus is the vine, I am the branch. If I abide in Him, then I'll be fruitful, but if I try to do everything on my own, I'll fail at what matters most. I need Him.

3. **Questions:**
   What does it mean to abide? How does Jesus abide in me? What kind of fruit is Jesus talking about?

4. **Cross-references:**
   John 6:56   "He that eats my flesh, and drinks my blood, abides in me, and I in him." This verse brings to mind the Eucharist, and the importance of receiving Christ in the Eucharist as often as possible. This is a very important way to abide in Jesus.

   John 15:7   "If you abide in me, and my words abide in you, ask for whatever you wish, and it will be done for you." How can Jesus' words abide in me if I never read them? I need to read the Bible if I want to abide in Christ.

   John 15:16   "It was not you who chose me, but I who chose you and appointed you to go and bear fruit that will remain, so that whatever you ask the Father in my name he may give you." Not all fruit remains. Some is good only temporarily—on earth. I want my fruit to remain in eternity—to count in the long run.

   Galatians 5:22–23   "The fruit of the Spirit is love, joy, peace, patience, kindness, generosity, faithfulness, gentleness, self-control." These are some of the fruits that will be seen if I abide in Christ.

5. **Personal Application:**

I will study my calendar this week, making note of where I spend my time. Is most of my time spent on things that will last for eternity (fruit that remains)? I'll reassess my priorities in light of what I find.

 NOTES

Appendix 3
CONVERSION OF HEART

The Catholic faith is full of beautiful traditions, rituals, and sacraments. As powerful as they are, it is possible for them to become mere habits in our lives, instead of experiences that draw us close to the heart of Christ. In the words of John Paul II, they can become acts of "hollow ritualism." We might receive our first Communion and the sacraments of confession and confirmation, yet never experience the interior conversion that opens the heart to a personal relationship with God.

Pope Benedict XVI has explained that the "door of faith" is opened at one's baptism, but we are called to open it again, walk through it, and rediscover and renew our relationship with Christ and His Church.[44]

So how do we do this? How do we walk through that door of faith so we can begin to experience the abundant life that God has planned for us?

GETTING PERSONAL

The word *conversion* means "the act of turning." This means that conversion involves a turning away from one thing and a turning toward another. When you haven't experienced conversion of heart, you are turned *toward* your own desires. You are the one in charge, and you do what you feel is right and best at any given moment. You may choose to do things that are very good for other people, but the distinction is that *you are choosing.* You are deciding. You are the one in control.

Imagine driving a car. You are sitting in the driver's seat, and your hands are on the steering wheel. You've welcomed Jesus into the passenger's seat, and have listened to His comments. But whether or not you follow His directions is really up to you. You may follow them or you may not, depending on what seems right to you.

When you experience interior conversion, you decide to turn, to get out of the driver's seat, move into the passenger's seat, and invite God to be the driver. Instead of seeing Him as an advice giver or someone nice to have around for the holidays, you give Him control of every aspect of your life.

More than likely, you don't find this easy to do. This is because of the universal struggle with pride. We want to be the ones in charge. We don't like to be in

---

[44] Pope Benedict XVI, *Apostolic Letter: Porta Fidei,* for the Indiction of the Year of Faith, October 11, 2011.

desperate need. We like to be the captains of our ships, charting our own courses. As William Ernest Henley wrote, "I am the master of my fate: I am the captain of my soul."

Conversion of heart isn't possible without humility. The first step is to recognize your desperate need of a savior. Romans 6:23 states that the "wages of sin is death." When you hear this, you might be tempted to justify your behavior, or compare yourself with others. You might think to yourself, "I'm not a murderer. I'm not as bad as this or that person. If someone were to put my good deeds and bad deeds on a scale, my good ones would outweigh the bad. So surely I am good enough? Surely I don't deserve death!" When this is your line of thought, you are missing a very important truth: Just one mortal sin is enough to separate you from a holy God. Just one mortal sin is enough for you to deserve death.[45] Even your best efforts to do good fall short of what God has required in order for you to spend eternity with Him. Isaiah 64:6 says, "All our righteous acts are like filthy rags." If you come to God thinking that you are going to be accepted by Him based on your "good conduct," He will point out that your righteousness is nothing compared to His infinite holiness.

Saint Thérèse of Lisieux understood this well, and wrote, "In the evening of my life I shall appear before You with empty hands, for I do not ask You to count my works. All our justices are stained in Your eyes. I want therefore to clothe myself in Your own justice and receive from Your love the eternal possession of Yourself."[46]

She recognized that her works, her best efforts, wouldn't be enough to earn salvation. Salvation cannot be earned. It's a free gift. Saint Thérèse accepted this gift, and said that if her justices or righteous deeds were stained, then she wanted to clothe herself in Christ's own justice. We see this described in 2 Corinthians 5:21: "God made him who had no sin to be sin for us, so that in him we might become the righteousness of God."

How did God make Him who had no sin to be sin for you? This was foretold by the prophet Isaiah: "But he was pierced for our transgressions, he was crushed for our iniquities; the punishment that brought us peace was upon him, and by his wounds we are healed" (Isaiah 53:5).

---

[45] One sin was enough to merit death for the first human beings who were in the state of preternatural perfection. For us, joined to Christ in His Body, one mortal sin merits death. Venial sin does not, although venial sin makes it easier to commit mortal sin. See CCC #1854-#1864.

[46] Saint Thérèse of Lisieux, "Act of Oblation to Merciful Love," June 9, 1895.

Jesus accomplished this on the cross. Every sin committed, past, present, and future, was placed on Him. Now, *all the merits of Jesus can be yours*. He wants to fill your empty hands with His own virtues.

But first, you need to recognize, just as Saint Thérèse did, that you are little. You are weak. You fail. You need forgiveness. You need a savior.

When you come before God in prayer and acknowledge these truths, He looks at your heart. He sees your desire to trust Him, to please Him, to obey Him. He says to you, "My precious child, you don't have to pay for your sins. My Son, Jesus, has already done that for you. He suffered, so that you wouldn't have to. I want to experience a relationship of intimacy with you. I forgive you.[47] Jesus came to set you free.[48] When you open your heart to me, you become a new creation![49] The old you has gone. The new you is here. If you will stay close to me, and journey by my side, you will begin to experience a transformation that brings joy and freedom.[50] I've been waiting to pour my gifts into your soul. Beloved daughter of mine, remain confident in me. I am your loving Father. Crawl into my lap. Trust me. Love me. I will take care of everything."

This is conversion of heart. This act of faith lifts the veil from your eyes and launches you into the richest and most satisfying life. You don't have to be sitting in church to do this. Don't let a minute pass before opening your heart to God and inviting Him to come dwell within you. Let Him sit in the driver's seat. Give Him the keys to your heart. Your life will never be the same again.

---

[47] "If we acknowledge our sins, he is faithful and just and will forgive our sins and cleanse us from every wrongdoing." 1 John 1:9

[48] "So if the Son makes you free, you will be free indeed." John 8:36

[49] "So whoever is in Christ is a new creation: the old things have passed away; behold, new things have come." 2 Corinthians 5:18

[50] "I will sprinkle clean water over you to make you clean; from all your impurities and from all your idols I will cleanse you. I will give you a new heart, and a new spirit I will put within you. I will remove the heart of stone from your flesh and give you a heart of flesh." Ezekiel 36:25–26

NOTES

Appendix 4
TIME MANAGEMENT TIPS

A good starting point for managing your time wisely is your desk. What does the top of your desk look like? Are you surrounded by a sea of papers and knickknacks? How many times does a paper get handled before it finds a home?

To begin to tame the chaos, gather the following supplies:

- Medium-size box
- Laundry basket
- Manila folder labeled "Task List"
- Manila folder labeled "Action Items"
- Pad of paper

STEP 1
Begin by filling the box with anything on your desk that doesn't have a home.

STEP 2
Take each item out of the box, one at a time, and find a place for it.

Does it go in the trash? Throw it away.

Does it belong in another part of the house? Put it in the laundry basket to be put away at the end of this exercise.

Does it require you to do something? Decide how much time is needed. If it can be accomplished in less than five minutes, do it now. If it can be accomplished in less than half an hour, put it in the folder marked "Task List," and then write the task down on the pad of paper. Place a due date next to the task. If it needs more than half an hour, assign a specific time for that task on your calendar, and put it in the folder labeled "Action Items."

STEP 3
Going forward: Assign a block of time *every day* to work on your task list. Ideally this is a set time that you protect for this purpose. You may prefer to spend a half hour in the morning and another half hour in the evening working through your list. Or you might prefer to spend an hour without interruption. Put this on your calendar as you

would any other appointment. Pay attention to the due dates associated with each task, doing the most time-sensitive items first.

STEP 4

Resist the urge to continually answer e-mails throughout the day. Constantly checking and answering e-mails causes countless tasks to be interrupted and done in a far less efficient way. It also communicates to the people around us that they are less important than our phones and computers. If someone has something truly urgent that he or she has e-mailed to you, that person will likely have your phone number and can call you to let you know.

When you sit down to answer your e-mails, try to do it at your computer instead of on the phone. Treat e-mails as you would the mail or any other item on your desk. Read an e-mail and determine how much time is required to answer it. If it's five minutes or less, take care of it right away. If it requires less than half an hour, print it out, put it in the Task List folder, and add it to your Task List. If it requires more than half an hour, print it out, put it in the Action Item folder, and put it on your calendar.

When we give our full attention to a task, our productivity and effectiveness increase. Multitasking is actually a time waster. Doug Merrill, author of *Getting Organized in the Google Era*, writes the following:

> When you're trying to accomplish two dissimilar tasks, each one requiring some level of consideration and attention, multitasking falls apart. Your brain just can't take in and process two simultaneous, separate streams of information and encode them fully into short-term memory. When information doesn't make it into short-term memory, it can't be transferred into long-term memory for recall later. If you can't recall it, you can't use it. And, presumably, you are trying to learn something from whatever you are doing, right? Instead of actually helping you, multitasking works against you. It's making you less efficient, not more.[51]

In addition to helping us work smarter, doing one thing at a time benefits those we love most. Instead of half-listening, we are fully present in the moment. This helps us to love, and that is the measure of true success.

---

[51] Douglas Merrill, "Why Multitasking Doesn't Work," *Forbes*, August 17, 2012, http://www.forbes.com/sites/douglasmerrill/2012/08/17/why-multitasking-doesnt-work/.

Answer Key

NOTES

Lesson 1, Day One

1. Personal reflection.
2. We don't worship God because He's lacking something or needs something from us. God is utterly complete in Himself. We don't sustain Him through our worship; rather, He sustains us through His moment-by-moment decision to give us breath and life.
3. We act this way when we question God—as if He owes us an explanation for the way He does things.
4. Our thoughts are not the same as God's thoughts. His are far beyond ours. Just because we don't understand something God has willed or allowed doesn't mean there isn't a good reason. We just don't see things from the same perspective or with the same wisdom as God.

Lesson 1, Day Two

1. Moses was allowed to see God's glory. When he asked for this great blessing, God granted his request, but said that no one could see His face and live. God said He would let His goodness pass before Moses, and would protect him at the same time. God set Moses in the cleft of a rock and covered him with His hand until He had passed by. He allowed Moses to see His back.
2. Moses was shining as a result of God's reflected glory. This made the people afraid to come near him, so he put a veil over his face.
3. The veil blocking access to God's presence in the Holy of Holies was split in two from top to bottom. This was done by God—no human hand could have torn it. The barrier between man and God had been torn down through Christ's sacrifice on the cross.
4. Answers will vary.

Lesson 1, Day Three

1. Whenever a person turns to the Lord, the veil is lifted.
2. When we gaze on the Lord's glory with an unveiled face, we're transformed into the image of Christ.
3. Answers will vary.
4. The sacraments and Eucharistic adoration are unique Catholic opportunities to gaze on the Lord's glory and enjoy His presence.

Lesson 1, Day Four

1. The four living creatures (angels that appear as animals) all chanted, "Holy, holy, holy, is the Lord God Almighty, who was and is and is to come!" (Revelation 4:8) We call this the Sanctus, and we pray it before receiving the Eucharist: "And so, with the Angels and all the Saints we declare your glory, as with one voice we acclaim: Holy, Holy, Holy Lord God of hosts. Heaven and earth are full of your glory. . . ."
2. The saints fell down, prostrate before God, and cast their crowns before the throne.
3. Saint Paul described his reward in heaven as a "crown of righteousness." "The image alludes to the garland or victory wreath used to crown winning athletes in the ancient Olympics (1 Cor 9:25)."[52]

---

[52] Ibid., 400.

4. Answers will vary.

Lesson 1, Day Five
1. We're told to pray constantly.
2. Answers will vary.
3. Answers will vary.
4. We are to offer our bodies as a living sacrifice.

Lesson 2, Day One
1. The earth and all it holds belongs to God. The world belongs to God, as do all the people who live in it.
2. We arrived in this world naked and with nothing in our possession. Everything we have has been given to us by God. Every good and perfect gift finds its source in Him. There's nothing we have that we can take credit for. Yes, we may have worked very hard for what we have—but who gave us the ability to work hard? Everything is a gift.
3. Answers will vary.
4. Answers will vary.

Lesson 2, Day Two
1. Answers will vary.
2. This verse encourages us to watch carefully how we live, making the most of every opportunity. This is a picture of a prayerful approach to where we spend time. We're encouraged to use our time to draw closer to God and spiritually encourage each other. We're to avoid time wasters. Getting drunk is a clear example of wasted time. We may justify that it's fun and just how we relax at a party, but the truth is, it takes time we could spend growing deeper in meaningful relationships and spends it on meaningless interactions that have no long-term value. The same could be said for drinking too much at home. When we reach a point that we aren't sharp and at our best due to alcohol, we are going to miss opportunities to build better relationships with our families. It often wastes time the following day when we are operating at half-mast due to a headache.
3. There is a time or season for everything in life, but not everything should be done in one season. We are wise to take stock of all our commitments, prayerfully considering the possibility that we are trying to do in one season of life what God would prefer we wait and do in another season.
4. Answers will vary.

Lesson 2, Day Three
1. Answers will vary.
2. Answers will vary.
3. Answers will vary.

Lesson 2, Day Four
1. **Romans 8:16** The Holy Spirit within us reminds us who we are. He reminds us that we are God's beloved daughters. When we read in John 16:8 that the Holy Spirit convicts us

of sin, it's a description of His work in our hearts, calling us to authenticity. He wants our behavior to match our true identity.

Romans 8:26 The Holy Spirit helps us in our weakness. When we don't know how or what to pray, the Holy Spirit intercedes for us.

Answers will vary.

2. **A.** The Holy Spirit dwells in the "inner self." He dwells inside the hearts of the children of God

   B. The Holy Spirit strengthens us with power.

   C. God wants us to have the strength to comprehend the breadth, length, height, and depth of the love Christ has for us. When we know and believe this in the depth of our being, we are filled with the fullness of God.

3. Unconfessed sin withers our strength. It also blocks our prayers. "If I had cherished iniquity in my heart, the Lord would not have listened." (Psalm 66:18)

Lesson 2, Day Five

1. Jesus told the disciples to get away by themselves and rest awhile.
2. CCC 2184 says that life should have a rhythm of work and rest. We weren't made to live like slaves. We were given the Lord's Day to cultivate our family, social, and spiritual lives. Sadly, most people are not experiencing this rhythm, existing to *do* rather than existing to *be*.
3. Answers will vary.
4. Choose this day whom you will serve. Are you going to be a slave to expectations—yours and others'—or are you going to decide to steward your time the way God wants you to? There isn't enough time in the day to keep everyone in your life happy. You have to choose.

Lesson 3, Day One

1. The Israelites were commanded to stop and rest on the Sabbath day. Stopping work would mean less would be produced, but in God's eyes, that wasn't what mattered most. It was far more important to God that His children receive the break that they needed and spend a day in His refreshing presence. It showed His care and concern for their well-being. It reminded them that they weren't cogs in a wheel. They were beloved, and God wanted them to experience the delight of rest.
2. Just like the Israelites in Egypt, we live in a culture in which our value is determined by what we do and what we produce. The Israelite slaves worked seven days a week, and so do we. Sunday has become a day like any other. We don't rest; we just trade one set of "to-dos" for another. Yet there is an important difference between the Israelites' lives and ours. While the Israelite slaves were forced to work in this way, we often have a choice. Most of us walk into this place of bondage by our own free will.
3. Answers will vary.
4. Answers will vary.

Lesson 3, Day Two

1. Sick and possessed people crowded around the house where Jesus stayed. This created a stir, and soon the whole town gathered to see what was going on. Jesus healed one

person after another and drove out demons. Undoubtedly, the people had never witnessed anything like this before. No doubt they would have hoped and expected that Jesus would do the same thing the next day. Whatever He was able to give, they would likely have wanted more—more healing, more teaching, more love. . . .

2. Jesus got up before dawn, left, and went to a deserted place to pray. Simon (Peter) and some others pursued Him and told Him that everyone was looking for Him. This was not an unusual way for Jesus to behave. According to Luke 5:15–16, "The report about [Jesus] spread all the more, and great crowds assembled to listen to him and to be cured of their ailments, but he would withdraw to deserted places to pray."

3. Jesus knew He had limited time—only three years of public ministry. The needs surrounding Him were great; there was no time to waste. Healings drew attention to Him, and as a result, to His message. Jesus had a compassionate heart, and the suffering of people trapped by illness or demon possession affected Him deeply. It must have been hard to leave when there were still people who needed healing.
Answers will vary.

4. God worked and created the heavens and earth in six days, but on the seventh day there was rest. This is the example we should follow.

Lesson 3, Day Three

1. In Matthew 18:3, Jesus tells us that we should become like children. Children are able to delight in simple things, and know how to play. We don't seem to have time to do those things, but a Sabbath day of rest allows us to delight in life without focusing on work.
2. Answers will vary.
3. Answers will vary.
4. We become more like Christ by being transformed into His likeness when we gaze on the glory of the Lord.

Lesson 3, Day Four

1. When we don't temper our desires, we are lured and enticed by them. We are tempted to covet what belongs to other people. The sin of covetousness "gives birth to death" (the death of contentment and rest).
2. Answers will vary.
3. Answers will vary.
4. Answers will vary.

Lesson 3, Day Five

1. Answers will vary.
2. Answers will vary.
3. Jeremiah 33:3 says that if we call to God, He will answer us—He'll tell us great things beyond the reach of our knowledge. Proverbs 3:5–6 reminds us that we shouldn't just rely on our own understanding of a situation. We should trust that God's wisdom is greater than ours, and invite Him to help us discern the right decisions every step of the way so He can show us the "straight path." James 1:5 promises us that if we ask God for wisdom, He will give it.

4. Proverbs 15:22 reminds us that our plans and decisions will be better if we've taken the time to seek guidance from wise people.

Lesson 4, Day One
1. God spoke to Moses face-to-face, as a person "speaks to a friend."
2. Moses asked God if he could see God's glory.
3. Answers will vary.
4. God told Moses that He was going to make His goodness pass before Him. He said that when His glory would pass by, He'd set Moses in the cleft of the rock and would cover him with His hand; beholding the fullness of God's glory would be too much for Moses.

Lesson 4, Day Two
1. Moses didn't know that the skin of his face had become radiant while he spoke with the Lord.
2. When we focus on the needs of others and how we can help them, we remove the focus from ourselves and reflect the care and concern of God (1 Corinthians 10:24). Instead of living for ourselves, we should live for Christ (2 Corinthians 5:15). If we stop comparing ourselves with and measuring ourselves against others, we'll have healthier self-images and be far less likely to be excessively self-focused (2 Corinthians 10:12).
3. In Matthew 16:24, we read that in order to be Jesus' followers, we must deny ourselves and pick up our crosses, and follow Him. This is far from being a terrible thing—we're told that if we will "lose our lives" for Christ's sake, we'll find genuine life in Him.

Lesson 4, Day Three
1. Jesus responded by asking the man a question and pointing him to the deeper issue at play.
2. The rich man financially planned for life before death, but he failed to plan for life after death.
3. When we accumulate more, we have the additional job of taking care of it and updating it. When we seek security and significance through our possessions, we'll spend our most precious resources on things that might matter temporarily, but will be meaningless in eternity.
4. Answers will vary.

Lesson 4, Day Four
1. Psalm 24:1–2 The earth is the Lord's. Just as with our time and possessions, God is the owner of the earth, and we are stewards. As stewards, we need to use what God has entrusted to us in a responsible way that would make Him pleased. God doesn't only care about the people He created; He also cares for His creation.
2. No. "This sovereignty is not to be an arbitrary and destructive domination. God calls man and woman, made in the image of the Creator 'who loves everything that exists,' to share in his providence toward other creatures; hence their responsibility for the world God has entrusted to them." (CCC 373)
3. Answers will vary.
4. Answers will vary.

Lesson 4, Day Five

1. God provided food and rest in a remote place.
2. The angel said that if Elijah didn't get up and eat, the journey would be too much for him.
3. God's voice was a light, silent sound; a gentle whisper; a still, small voice.
4. Answers will vary.

Lesson 5, Day One

1. We can trust Him because God is good.
   We can trust Him because God loves us.
2. "Not what I will but what you will." (Mark 14:36)
3. For Jesus, yielding to His Father's will meant the cross. It meant suffering through an unjust trial; being scourged, humiliated, betrayed; experiencing extreme physical pain; and then enduring the spiritual agony of separation from God. He didn't endure the cross passively; He actively chose God's will over His own comfort *for our sake*.
4. Answers will vary.

Lesson 5, Day Two

1. We have become God's slaves.
2. Jesus described surrender as similar to a grain of wheat falling to the ground and dying, but then later becoming a seed that produces more fruit. In that same way, when we surrender, dying to the things that we want instead of insisting upon them, holiness grows within our hearts. This holiness prepares us for eternal life with God in heaven.
3. We're to rejoice always. No matter what our circumstances, we're to thank God. The only way we can do this is by first arriving at a place where we recognize that everything that comes from God's hand has been permitted by Him for our good. When we have yielded our will and have prayed, "Your will be done," we can thank Him for whatever He sends, trusting that in His love, He would never send something to harm us.
4. Answers will vary.

Lesson 5, Day Three

1. We are to surrender our bodies to God. This means surrendering our desire for more sleep and getting up to pray. It means following God's plan for sexuality instead of what our culture says is acceptable. It means surrendering the longing to sit on the couch, eating whatever we want, and instead treating our bodies as temples of the Holy Spirit, eating well and exercising.
2. We are to surrender our minds. This means that we'll take the time to renew our minds, which goes beyond adjusting our behaviors. The very way that we think and what we think about needs to be transformed by God. What we feed our minds will shape us interiorly. God wants us to saturate our minds with His truth, contained in Scripture and the teachings of the Church. When we find time to numb the mind with television but don't have time to study and meditate on His words, we haven't fully surrendered our minds to God.
3. God wants us to surrender our hearts to Him.
4. Answers will vary.

Lesson 5, Day Four

1. When we can see things clearly, we don't need hope. We hope for what we can't see. We wait with endurance for something better to come. Hope is described in Hebrews 6:18–19 as a sure and firm anchor for the soul.
2. We are hoping for the good that God will bring out of our situation, no matter how bad the situation might be.
3. "Hope is expressed and nourished in prayer, especially in the Our Father." (CCC 1820)
4. Our focus should be on eternity. Although it doesn't seem to be true, life passes very quickly. The way we live today will determine the quality of our eternity. The joy of heaven will be worth every bit of suffering we may endure here on earth.

Lesson 5, Day Five

1. **Luke 1:25–28** Mary surrendered her reputation, her ideal betrothal period, her body, and her security.
   Luke 2:6-7 Mary surrendered her desire for the physical comfort of a home and the emotional comfort of women she knew by her side as she gave birth surrounded by animals.
   Luke 2:41-49 When Jesus was only twelve, it became clear that He would always seek to do God's will before anything else. This would mean a painful separation from His mother. Mary would have to release Jesus to His Father's hands time and time again.
2. Mary experienced the most difficult time of surrender as she stood at the foot of the cross, watching her precious Son suffer and die.
3. Answers will vary.
4. Answers will vary.

Lesson 6, Day One

1. We are told to think about things that are true, honorable, just, pure, lovely, gracious, excellent, and praiseworthy.
2. Worry isn't consistent with Philippians 4:8 because we aren't thinking about something that is true; rather, it's something that *might be* true. Critical thoughts about others aren't consistent with Philippians 4:8 because the thoughts aren't pure or lovely. Negative thoughts about yourself aren't consistent with Philippians 4:8 for the same reason. Malicious thoughts aren't honorable. Thoughts about the things we wish would change (discontent) aren't lovely or gracious.
3. Satan is described as a liar and the father of lies. He will tempt us to dwell on things that aren't true, by encouraging us to assume that we have the whole picture, therefore not giving people the benefit of the doubt; or by persuading us to focus on potential negative outcomes of things we're worrying about while diminishing the difference it makes when God is present in any situation. He'll tempt us to dwell on lies about ourselves, about things we've done that we're ashamed of, about present challenges we feel inadequate for. He'll whisper lies into our ears that we're not good enough, that we don't have what it takes to be holy, that God doesn't love us. Lies. Lies. Lies. This is his language.
4. Answers will vary.

Lesson 6, Day Two

1. When we engage in a supernatural battle, it's utterly different from a physical one. Our weapons are different from guns and swords. They are more powerful, capable of destroying fortresses. These fortresses aren't physical buildings; they are the places we go for security and safety instead of going to God. They need to be torn down so that we will go to the right place for healing and security. Much of this battle takes place inside us, in the mind and heart. We are told that we are to take every thought captive to Christ.
2. The armor and weapons that will help us fight our spiritual battles are truth, righteousness, the gospel, faith, salvation, and the sword of the Spirit (the Bible).
3. **Psalm 23:1** "The Lord is my shepherd, I shall not want."
   Isaiah 43:4 "You are precious in my eyes and honored, and I love you."
   1 Samuel 16:7 "God does not see as a mortal, who sees the appearance. The LORD looks into the heart."
   1 John 1:9 "If we acknowledge our sins, he is faithful and just and will forgive our sins and cleanse us from every wrongdoing."

Lesson 6, Day Three

1. We should guard what we look at.
2. We should guard whom we spend time with.
3. We should guard what we watch and listen to. We need to be careful to avoid gossip, and to be aware of the things that fill our minds with fear. If watching the news unsettles you, it makes sense to avoid it in the evening, when it's sure to affect your dreams and rest.
4. Answers will vary.

Lesson 6, Day Four

1. God promises to guard our hearts and minds with His peace. This peace surpasses human understanding. It's inexplicable apart from Him. But we're to bring our worries and requests to Him in a spirit of thanksgiving. Even as we lay out what we are worried about, we need to thank Him for the things He has done in the past and is doing for us in the future. This helps build trust in God in our hearts, which is the best antidote to worry.
2. The truth is that God has called me by name and I belong to Him. Even if my worst-case scenario occurs, He will be with me as I "pass through waters." He'll make sure that my worries won't overpower me and sweep me away. Even though it seems like I won't make it, God promises that I won't be consumed. We should never imagine the future without imagining His difference-making presence at the same time.
3. Ecclesiastes 7:14 tells us that we can't know the future, and CCC 2115 warns against trying to figure it out through divination. The future is in God's hands. As much as we'd like to see into the future and control it, that realm belongs only to God.
4. **John 16:33** We know that we'll have trouble. God never promised us a problem-free life. But we also know that Christ has conquered the world. He is more powerful than anything we can imagine, and His strength is enough to get us through even the most difficult circumstances.

Isaiah 41:10 God will strengthen us, help us, and uphold us. There is nothing we will face alone. And God will provide us with all we need.

Isaiah 54:10 No matter what happens, God's love will never be taken from us.

Jeremiah 29:11 God has a plan for our lives. It's not a plan to harm us. It's filled with hope and purpose. He has the power to bring that plan to fruition, no matter what obstacles we may face.

Lesson 6, Day Five

1. Dwelling on the past isn't helpful if there is no attempt made to forgive, heal, learn lessons, and move to a place of healing. Thinking about past events with a victim's mind-set leaves us in a very dark place, but when we address painful memories in light of God's unconditional love, we can look for any way that God has been at work, redeeming our lives from that point on and perhaps even in that very area of life that once was so painful.

2. Answers will vary.

3. So often, we don't know how deeply our actions will hurt others. We don't always know what we have done, and other people don't always know what the consequences of their actions will be. When we realize that hurting people hurt people, we are better able to offer grace. We realize that we're all broken and dealing with our own hurts.

4. These verses encourage us to take the comfort that we received from God during our painful times and pass it on to others who are in pain. What He poured into us can overflow into the lives of people who will be uniquely comforted by someone who knows how it feels to suffer. When you've "been there," your words of comfort carry extra weight.

NOTES

Prayer Pages

NOTES

The Grail Prayer

Lord Jesus,
I give You my hands to do Your work.
I give You my feet to go Your way.
I give You my eyes to see as You do.
I give You my tongue to speak Your words.
I give You my mind that You may think in me.
I give You my spirit that You may pray in me.
Above all, I give You my heart that You may love in me
Your Father and all mankind.
I give You my whole self that You may grow in me,
So that it is You, Lord Jesus,
Who live and work and pray in me.

Prayer Requests

Date:

Date:

Prayer Requests

Date:

Date:

Prayer Requests

Date:

Date:

 —————— NOTES ——————

NOTES

"For to the one who has, more will be given"
Matthew 13:12

CHRIST'S LOVE IS ENDLESS.

And the journey doesn't end here.

Walking With Purpose is more than a Bible study, it's a supportive community of women seeking lasting transformation of the heart. And you are invited.

Walking With Purpose believes that change happens in the hearts of women – and, by extension, in their families and beyond – through Bible study and community. We welcome all women, irrespective of faith background, age, or marital status.

Connect with us online for regular inspiration and to join the conversation. There you'll find insightful blog posts, Scriptures, and downloads.

For a daily dose of spiritual nourishment, join our community on Facebook, Twitter, Pinterest and Instagram.

And if you're so moved to start a Walking With Purpose study group at home or in your parish, take a look at our website for more information.

walkingwithpurpose.com
The Modern Woman's Guide to the Bible.

walking with purpose

NOTES

❋ DEEPEN YOUR FAITH ❋ OPEN YOUR ARMS ❋ ❋ BROADEN YOUR CIRCLE ❋

When your heart opens, and your love for Christ deepens, you may be moved to bring Walking With Purpose to your friends or parish. It's rewarding experience for many women who, in doing so, learn to rely on God's grace while serving Him.

If leading a group seems like a leap of faith, consider that you already have all the skills you need to share the Lord's Word:

- Personal commitment to Christ
- Desire to share the love of Christ
- Belief in the power of authentic, transparent community

The Walking With Purpose community supports you with:

- Training
- Mentoring
- Bible study materials
- Promotional materials

Few things stretch and grow our faith like stepping out of our comfort zone and asking God to work through us. Say YES, soon you'll see the mysterious and unpredictable ways He works through imperfect women devoted to Him.

Remember that if you humbly offer Him what you can, He promises to do the rest.

"See to it that no one misses the grace of God" Hebrews 12:15

Learn more about bringing Walking with Purpose to your parish.
Visit us at walkingwithpurpose.com
The Modern Woman's Guide To The Bible.

NOTES

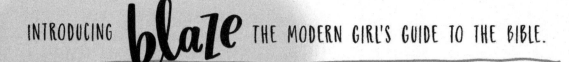

INTRODUCING *blaze* THE MODERN GIRL'S GUIDE TO THE BIBLE.

Do you want to help girls grow in confidence, faith, and kindness?

The Lord is calling for women like you to speak truth into the hearts of young girls – girls who are understandably confused about their true worth and beauty. Blaze is a fun and engaging program developed especially for 7th and 8th grade girls to counteract the cultural forces that drive them to question their value, purpose, and faith.

Like Walking With Purpose, Blaze makes the wisdom of the Bible relevant to today's challenges. Blaze teaches girls to recognize the difference between the loving, affirming voice of their heavenly Father and the voices that tell them they aren't good enough.

Would you like to be a positive influence on the girls you know? Start a Blaze program in in your parish or community.

It's easy and convenient to share God's word with a Leader's Guide and Blaze kit that includes:

- Blaze Prayer Journals
- Truth vs. Lie Cards
- Fun gifts for the girls
- Facebook and Instagram messaging to maintain connection and amplify the message

Additional resources to nurture girls' spiritual growth:

- Discovering My Purpose – a 6-session Bible study that leads girls on an exploration of their own spiritual gifts
- Between You & Me – a 40-day conversation guide for mothers and daughters

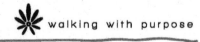

walking with purpose

For more spiritual inspiration or to learn more about Blaze and Walking With Purpose, visit us at walkingwithpurpose.com/BLAZE

You're also invited to join our community on Facebook, Twitter, Pinterest and Instagram.

"Be who God meant you to be and you will set the world on fire." - Saint Catherine of Siena

 NOTES

SPIRITUAL EXERCISES FOR STRENGTHENING YOUR FAITH

The *Opening Your Heart Series* is a three-part Bible Study created especially for young women, the beloved daughters of God.
Six lessons in each book invite you to explore and deepen your faith and your relationship with the Redeemer –
the One who loves you truly, unconditionally, and infinitely.

Beloved – *Part I*
Grace and practical tools to help you make your relationship with God your first priority.

Unshaken – *Part II*
How to bravely face challenges in your effort to follow Christ and live comfortably in the arms of His love.

Steadfast – *Part III*
Explore living without fear, your life purpose, your vocations, and the depth of God's personal love for you, his beloved daughter.

For more spiritual inspiration or to learn more about Walking With Purpose, visit us at walkingwithpurpose.com

walking with purpose

You're also invited to join our community on
Facebook, Twitter, Pinterest and Instagram.

walking with purpose

Mission

Walking with Purpose transforms the hearts
and lives of women by providing Bible studies
that enable women to know Christ
through Scripture and the teachings of the
Roman Catholic Church.

Vision

To enable every Catholic woman
in America to experience our life-changing
Bible study, **Opening Your Heart.**

Join us in transforming the hearts and lives of women.
Make a gift to Walking with Purpose today!

walkingwithpurpose.com/donate